LIVING WITH
CATS

LIVING WITH
CATS

GALE B. NEMEC

Quill
William Morrow
New York

It is the policy of William Morrow and Company, Inc., and its imprints and affiliates, recognizing the importance of preserving what has been written, to print the books we publish on acid-free paper, and we exert our best efforts to that end.

Library of Congress Cataloging-in-Publication Data
Nemec, Gale B.
    Living with cats / Gale B. Nemec
        p. cm.
    Includes bibliographical references and index.
    ISBN 0-688-10022-8
    1. Cats.   I. Title.
SF447.N46 1993
636.8—dc20   92-25706
                                               CIP

Printed in the United States of America

First Quill Edition

1 2 3 4 5 6 7 8 9 10

BOOK DESIGN BY GLEN M. EDELSTEIN

This book is dedicated
to the love and family
that surrounds

Joy
Debi
James
Francie
Ruthie
Mary
Ruth
Jim
Jan
Jay
Jean
Jim

May God hold you all
in his loving arms forever

information from how to choose a cat, to traveling with cats, to clipping your cat's toenails. We have included interviews and anecdotes with celebrities who were guests on the program as well as from people who have written to the program.

This is a book you will enjoy, learn from, and refer to almost daily and it includes two personal sections for you and your cat: a household hazards chart and a medical records chart.

Living with Cats would not have been possible without the contributions of many people to whom I am deeply grateful: Jamie Maurey, my exceptional producer; Michael Brim from the Cat Fanciers' Association, who supplied us with invaluable information; Dr. Bruce Herwald, Rosemary Reed, Joy Werner, Judy Peizer, Donna and John Todhunter, and Jon Spradley—all cat lovers who contributed personal cat stories and their time; James Nemec, Jr., and his wonderful talents; Peggy Miller and Paul Mahon, whose friendship and advice were invaluable; Tom Werner and Joseph Spies, photographers whose photographs are proof of their incredible talent; Larry Johnson, our terrific cat breed photographer; Mick Herkner, Mary Eno, Ann Marie Maier, Debbie Duel, and Linda Willen, who have devoted their careers to homeless animals in the metropolitan Washington, D.C., area and also selected cats and kittens from area shelters to be photographed for our cover. Makeup artist Terry Maki and hairstylist Robin Weir; Sonny Bloch, who threw me into animal programing; Lucy McNair, Margie Hugh, Idy Marcus, and Pat Carlile; Scruffette and Curmudgeon Cattywhompus; all of the animal experts who have been guests on *Living with Animals;* my parents, Jim and Ruth Nemec, who had the brilliant foresight to have me in the first place, and of course all of my siblings, cousins, nieces, and nephews, including the Tyners, Spradleys, Doremuses, Heards, Mathesons, all twenty-three of them and counting; and Bill Proctor, who guided me and worked with me to create this book, and finally for the blessings gained from the experience of *Living with Cats*.

And mostly my gratitude goes to you, the readers, and to the viewers of *Living with Animals*. I thank you for buying *Living with Cats*. I know you will enjoy having it as a reference and giving it as a gift to your cat-loving friends and relatives.

Our fragile lives are made up of memories and of moments in time. Remind yourself to live life an hour at a time—it's actually all we have. Relish each minute—the ups and the downs. Appreciate your time as you live it, acknowledge your life as it *actually* is, and not what you *think* it is.

Lastly—enjoy the unique relationship you share living with your cat!

Thanks!

Contents

CHAPTER ONE

WHAT'S LIFE WITHOUT A CAT?

WITH CATS I NEVER KNOW QUITE WHAT TO EXPECT. I've encountered numerous cats on my television show, *Living with Animals,* but there are no duplications. Each has his or her own special quirks, sensitivities, and tastes, and this endless variety and potential for surprise are what I love about the cat population.

My own interest in cats began at a very early age. As one of seven children, I didn't experience a time when there weren't several cats or dogs living in our home. People actually used to drive by our house and leave their cats in our yard because they heard we were unreserved cat lovers. They were right. Every cat that came through our doors was showered with love and attention—though I certainly have never recommended abandoning any animal in an-

Gale respectfully sits next to a wild Bengal tiger at Shambala Preserve in California. BILL DOW/ SHAMBALA PRESERVE

other person's front yard. Currently, my live-in cat is a male mixed-breed called Curmudgeon, or "Crudge" for short, who happens to be sitting behind me on *my* chair.

Despite my personal background with these animals, every time I'm introduced to a cat or cat owner, something unique or memorable seems to happen, though at the time the experiences don't always seem so cute or funny. My stomach, hands, and arms have been clawed, and my blouse ripped during interviews. I have been hissed at, braved bared teeth, and lived in fear of being bitten or even ripped apart, but so far I've escaped serious injury. I've developed a variety of techniques for calming frightened cats. Or failing that, I'm sometimes forced just to let them run around the set. In fact on one occasion we ended up taping an interview with the owner while the cat hid under a ladder.

I've introduced cats to dogs who have never met a cat, with decidedly mixed results. Sometimes the two have gotten along like long-lost relatives at a family reunion; sometimes they've just ignored each other. And sometimes I've had to help separate a scared and cowering feline from an overly aggressive canine "catter," who would like nothing better than to take a bite out of his fellow animal guest.

Some of these creatures have been common alley cats or graduates of animal shelters. Others have been pure-bred upper-crust show animals that are the pride of their owners and judges in the Cat Fanciers' Association. I even met the first test-tube kitten, who was born at the National Zoo in Washington, D.C.

As for the *wild* kind of cat, I've stroked a lion, observed up-close white Bengal tigers frolicking in the water, and conducted an interview with a baby cheetah and its keeper from Cypress Gardens, Florida. (That time the keeper got clawed, not me!)

One common thread in these experiences is that in every case I've learned something new. For example I learned that Scott Hamilton, the Olympic Gold Medalist figure-skating champion, has a cat that *loves* water. In interviewing dozens of veterinarians, I've learned it's practically impossible to find a doctor who recommends milk for cats; in fact they all say milk is bad for our feline friends.

And I learned from the crooner Perry Como that cats may love to take walks in the evening, just like dogs—an insight that adds a whole new meaning to the term *catwalk*.

Olympic gold medalist Scott Hamilton shows Gale photos of his favorite feline. Because of a previous appointment, Scott's cat couldn't join them for the interview.   ALLAN WEDERTZ

A Real Cat Walk

I may be a bit behind the times, but I never realized that some cats, like most dogs, like to take their owners for walks. The singer Perry Como has this perfectly groomed, pure-white cat with deep-blue eyes. The animal looks more like he belongs in some regal throne room than in the great outdoors. Yet this feline is definitely not a stay-at-home type.

"He insists on going for walks every night around six P.M.," Perry said.

This preference for a daily constitutional has become something of a family tradition. The cat scratches the door when it's time, the family follows him out of the house, down the street, and across intersections. More than one motorist does a double take at this parade, and several slow down, apparently to guard against an unpredictable bolt or sideways move by the cat. In fact Perry told me he, too, was worried that the cat might someday dart out into the road and be hit by a motorist. Now it was my turn to fill him in on an important cat fact: "You know, there are cat leashes," I said.

"You're kidding."

"Nope. I'll get you one."

So I went out and bought him a cat leash, a blue one to match his cat's blue eyes. Cat leashes, by the way, are different from dog leashes. They're constructed like a harness so that one part goes across the back and another crisscrosses around the front legs and chest.

That's another thing I had to learn about cats. As a rule they simply should not wear traditional dog collars.

One reason that most cautious cats and savvy owners don't like dog collars is that historically these devices have been detrimental (to put it mildly) to feline health. The problem is these solid collars have been responsible for many cats being strangled. The animal will get out in the yard and start chasing something or climbing a tree, and then the *collar* will catch on a branch. Many cats have died during such accidents because they couldn't get out of their collars. These same types of accidents occur in the home as well.

An alternative, in addition to the harness, is a cat collar with one segment made of elastic that can stretch when the collar catches on something. These are much safer because the cat can usually squirm around, pull free, and escape before he chokes.

Another reason that so many cats literally die from their collars is that well-meaning owners forget that a kitten is in the process of growing. As she gets bigger, so does her neck size. Many times the cat outgrows the collar without the owner's ever realizing what's happened. The cat can also get too large for the collar if she gains weight.

Consequently collars—even those with elastic segments—should be checked frequently in cats of all ages to be sure that the device hasn't become so tight that it's strangling the animal.

Cats Are People Too!

I suppose that living with cats is a lot like living with kids. Almost every time you're with them, you're in for a surprise. They are constantly showing you more about themselves and teaching you more about *yourself*.

For example, most humans get a little nervous before they appear on a television show. I mean, I do this for a living, and even *I* get nervous. (So now the truth is out, though I like to refer euphemistically to my anxious response as "a release of high energy.") The heart begins to pump harder; the throat gets dry; and whatever twitches or tics may be lying dormant soon begin to surface.

It's the same with cats. You may have the calmest cat around—that is, until he is thrust into an unfamiliar studio scene, with bright lights, cameras, and all sorts of strange people and sounds bouncing back and forth. When the show starts, all sorts of weird things can happen.

Jean LeClerc, the number-one sex symbol on daytime television, was waiting with his long-haired Himalayan, Kismet, in the green room, the place where guests sit just before they are interviewed on camera. The green room is pleasantly appointed at normal room temperature, but the atmosphere changes dramatically when the guests walk into the studio. The temperature is kept around 55° to allow the sensitive cameras and other machinery to func-

Jean LeClerc from the soap opera *All My Children* and his beautiful Himalayan, Kismet. A little intimidated by "lights, camera, action," Kismet shed everywhere!

tion properly. Also, the lights are *very* bright to maximize the video quality, which consequently make the studio very hot.

Just as a human guest may begin to feel a little on edge before a good performance, the cat also gets edgy. That is, in fact, an understatement. These animals can get so nervous that they often begin to shed—and that's exactly what happened to Kismet. Before we had talked for more than a few seconds on camera, cat hair was everywhere!

Jean tried hard to project his usual relaxed, sexy image, and he did succeed in giving the impression of being smooth and classy, but it wasn't easy. As the interview progressed, so much hair came off the animal's coat that Jean actually seemed to be swimming in the stuff. At the same time that he answered my questions, he was, more often than not, picking hair off the end of his nose, out of his ears, and out of his mouth. To make matters worse, Kismet didn't even want to sit on Jean's lap, and so he had to apply some firm wrestling holds to keep the pet in place.

Actually Jean handled the whole thing quite well, considering the circusmtances. Several times he said, "I can't believe this. My cat never sheds this way." But still, he managed to respond without a hitch in that creamy French accent—as he gently manhandled the cat with his left hand and tried to get rid of the hair with his right.

Many animals who are making a first-time appearance in this high-pressure setting shed hair as Jean's cat did. (For all I know, humans do too!) The cause is nerves. But when an animal has become more accustomed to the media attention, the opposite can occur. He can become so relaxed that he falls asleep!

That's what often happens now with my dog, Scruffette, the super-star animal-shelter graduate, who frequently appears on our show. She's so used to the lights and the action that she may nod off just before we're ready to do an interview. More than once the director has barked, "Gale, please wake up Scruffette. She looks like she's dead!" At that point I usually change Scruffette's position and she purrs comfortably (yes, dogs do purr!).

Undoubtedly the same lazy and even jaded attitude would overtake any cat who becomes a regular TV star—witness the aplomb of Morris the Cat, the peddler of 9-Lives cat food in the TV commercials.

There are many similarities between cats and humans, and there are also many examples that remind us how important cats are in our culture.

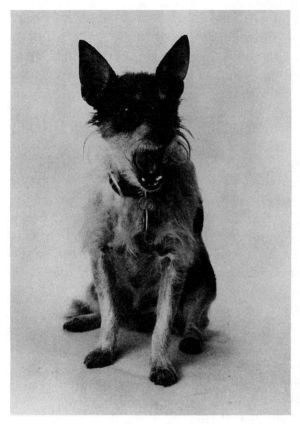

Scruffette, the super-
star shelter dog, pre-
tending she's the cat's
meow.

Cat Facts

Too often cats are the butt of comments that would make
any human boil with righteous indignation. Those who
aren't living with a cat often see these animals as rather
sinister creatures, in the tradition of the bad-luck black cat.
Even though the cat was once held in high esteem by the
Egyptians, cat-related terms such as *fat cat, cattiness,* or the
cat-o'-nine-tails are associated with mean-spirited or even
evil intentions. Even children are introduced to negative
cat images at Halloween with the traditional witch's evil

black cat and in such films as the Disney classic *The Lady and the Tramp*. In that movie two of the most insidious "bad guys" are the slimy Siamese cats who engage in dirty tricks as they sing, "We are Siamese if you please. We are Siamese if you *don't* please."

But perhaps the ultimate popular personification of the evil cat is the zombie feline featured in Stephen King's horror novel *Pet Sematary*. This animal, which keeps coming back from the dead, becomes a hideous repository of wickedness and danger.

Let's get rid of these negative cat images once and for all! It's time to forsake such inaccurate and defamatory myths and recognize the benign and constructive facts about today's cat. To this end cat lovers may want to file away in their memories the following special pieces of information, which demonstrate unequivocally that cats are the superior and dominant pet: especially to their owners.

- *Cats* are really man's best friend. Some evidence: They are the most popular companion animal in the United States, with 57 to 59 million animals owned by more than 27 million households. Dogs come in second with 55 to 57 million.
- An amazing 42 percent of pet-owning households have two or more cats.
- Not only are cats the top pet, they have been invading our homes at an incredibly rapid rate. In 1982, for instance, there were 43.9 million cats kept as pets. That number soared to nearly 58 million by 1987.
- People who rent are more likely to have a cat than a dog. (Now there's a great icebreaker at a cocktail party!)

- Cats are real people, just like most of us.
  The majority of cats owned as pets—53 percent—are mixed breeds, while only 8 percent are purebred.
- Younger heads of households, age twenty-
  five to forty-four years, and elderly women
  are more likely to have cats as pets.

As the popularity of cats has increased, so has the desire
for practical information that can promote the health and
happiness of the animal, as well as the pet's friendship with
the human. Living with cats over the years and now working with them, I have been in the fortunate position to
observe and learn a great deal with numerous feline experts. This book, which has been inspired by these observations and interviews, includes both the tidbits of
information that will make your cat happier and healthier
and also the broader concerns that will enhance the cat-
human relationship. It's a blueprint for living with cats
and loving them with abandon.

Here's a sampling of the information you'll find in the
following pages:

- Which purr suits your personality? How to
  buy a cat.
- Cats and kids.
- Cats and the elderly.
- Cats for dog lovers—including which cats
  act most like dogs.
- Aerobics for cats—including some specific
  exercise suggestions. No fat cats in this
  book!!
- Training your cat at your own "Feline U."
- Teaching your cat to learn to "heel" and do
  other dog tricks.

- Physical sanctions: In training, does it help to use squirt guns or even a cuff with the hand?
- Ways to cat-proof your home.
- Medical tips to alert you to potential physical and emotional problems common to cats so that you can call the vet without delay.
- Ways to prevent diseases that may threaten the health of your pet.
- What to do about cat-related allergies.
- Deciding if your cat needs therapy.
- A guide to help caring owners engage in proper feeding and grooming.
- Understanding how milk can kill cats.
- The pros and cons of neutering and declawing.
- Nine lives—myth or reality?
- Cat equipment and supplies, including litter-boxes, sitting services, and gourmet foods.
- Living with the death of a cat—and helping a cat deal with the death of another animal or human.

Now, let's begin at the very beginning—with an exploration of how to select a cat that will fit your personality perfectly.

CHAPTER TWO

WHICH PURR SUITS YOUR PERSONALITY?

HIS HOME? An elementary school in Los Angeles. His name? Room 8, because that's where, year after year, the members of a sixth-grade class cared for him and enjoyed him.

Room 8, a large gray tomcat, first walked into the Elysian Heights Elementary School in 1952. Nobody knew where he came from or whether he had ever had a previous owner—certainly his independent ways and obvious self-assurance indicated that he didn't particularly *need* an owner—but because he liked the kids in that particular sixth-grade class, he decided to stick around—year, after year, after year.

At first the teacher wasn't so sure about the advisability of encouraging a strange feline intruder. But the children insisted, and the teacher finally agreed that so long as the visitor didn't cause trouble, he could stay.

This open-door policy provided Room 8 with a quite literal window of opportunity: He entered the classroom every day over one of the windowsills. Before long the children had stocked up on some cat food and set up a cat feeder, though as often as not, Room 8 headed directly for the cat food shelf when he got hungry.

Room 8's sense of timing was uncanny (even uncatty?). His first year he disappeared in June on the last day of school. Nobody knew where he went, though many students, and more than one teacher, wondered sadly if they would ever see him again. But this cat knew a good thing when he saw it. He showed up a few months later on the very first day of classes. It didn't seem to bother him that a new sixth-grade group was there to greet him. Without missing a beat, he settled right in with the strange students and resumed his regular routine of eating and socializing. In fact by this time he knew more about the Room 8 than they did!

Room 8 took his regular summer vacations and returned with a new set of kids every year until 1968. His life and times became legendary as *Look* magazine and various TV stations recorded his activities. This once-stray cat became so famous that children he had never met wrote him piles of letters.

Even more important, as the school's principal said, "He started a tradition of loving animals in our school. Now we have a barnyard, with goats, sheep, and bunny rabbits, all cared for by the children. Room 8 really showed us how to love animals."

This special cat died in 1968, and on a memorial wall at the school, children drew paws and pictures and left affectionate notes. One little girl wrote on a slab of concrete a permanent message for posterity: "He slept on my desk."

**Morris the cat—need
we say more?**

The story of Room 8 touches me at a deep level. Having
had several cats at one time or another, I know that it's
essential to find just the right human-feline match for these
independent, often aloof, but still sensitive and intelligent
creatures. There's a particular "purr" out there that suits
your personality, but finding the right cat isn't an easy task.
So where do you start?

Should You Rely on the Shelter Solution?

I'm a big advocate of beginning the search for the perfect
cat in the local animal shelter. Cats with Room 8's special,
endearing personality traits can be found there if you just
know how to conduct your search.

As the story goes, Morris the Cat, of TV commercial
fame, was discovered in just such a shelter. He was a stray,

wandering the streets of an unnamed New England town when he was picked up and put into the shelter. It's unclear exactly who discovered Morris and rescued him from the shelter. In any case he was adopted by 9-Lives cat food and became their spokescat, under the watchful eye of a show-biz rep, Bob Martwick. Morris moved in with Martwick in west suburban Chicago, where the cat made his home in a cardboard box underneath Bob's desk.

The experience of Morris is a high-profile lesson in how a superior cat can be found in animal shelters—*if* you know what to look for. Here are some of the key considerations as you consider a potential catmate:

- The eyes should be bright and clear, with no discharge, including the area at the corners of the eyes near the nose.
- The nose shouldn't be runny.
- The coat should be shiny and full, with no bare patches.
- The cat should *not* sit huddled away in a corner. That sort of behavior can indicate illness. Rather, he should come up close to you and perhaps purr.
- A playful, frisky, happy cat is preferable to a shy, reticent one. However, the final choice is up to you.
- The color of the gums should be pink, not white.
- Any odd behavior, such as frequent urination, can indicate illness.

Male or Female?   Whether you get a male or female cat, the pet should be spayed (have the ovaries removed) or neutered (have the testes removed). Those unfamiliar with cats may find such advice off-putting. But experienced cat lovers know that this procedure is essential, both to prevent the birth of new kittens that simply can't be cared for, sold or adopted and also to eliminate aggressive or other unsociable behavior associated with feline sexuality.

The cost of spaying or neutering is minimal and can be taken care of at the animal shelter. If the shelter doesn't have the facilities to perform this simple operation, they will recommend a vet in your area.

Once this procedure has been done, the choice between a male and female is mostly a matter of personal preference. Some cat experts have suggested that in general, females tend to be more aloof and wary, while males are more personable. On the other hand, even after they are neutered, some males may tend to "spray," or urinate outside the litter box to establish territorial claims. Such habits are a matter of individual peculiarities and usually can't be predicted before you choose the cat.

Longhair or Shorthair?   Shorthaired cats are less trouble to groom than longhairs. But many owners are so taken with the beauty of a longhaired cat that they enjoy the daily comb-outs and grooming. This procedure not only removes the knots in the cat's coat but also establishes a unique human-animal bond between the cat and its owner.

You'll have to decide in advance whether you're cut out to be a "no-fuss" owner or one who prefers to spend time grooming your pet.

Millions of shelter cats have found new homes through such programs as Adopt-a-Cat Month, an annual placement program sponsored by the American Humane Association, more than one thousand animal shelters, and the 9-Lives cat food company. This program alone has enabled more than 1.5 million shelter cats to find permanent homes.

A major advantage of going to a shelter for your pet is that you can often find just the right cat while spending very little money. You may even discover a purebred cat—and you will automatically save a cat's life. An estimated seven out of ten cats in shelters are subjected to euthanasia (mercy killing) because there simply isn't enough space to handle them.

Note: Don't think shelters are willing to give an animal to just anyone. Today many of these facilities have implemented a policy known as the "home check." This involves sending a representative of the shelter to a prospective owner's home to see where the cat will be living. The reason for this procedure is to ensure that there will be enough space for the animal, and that the animal will be taken care of properly.

Finally, when you adopt your new feline friend, be sure that you have an agreement with the shelter that allows you to have the cat checked by a vet before your ownership becomes permanent. This way, if the cat isn't healthy, you'll be able to return it to the shelter and get either a refund or another cat.

The shelter may also want *you* to sign an agreement. For example, as part of the adoption arrangement you may have to guarantee that you will have your cat spayed or neutered within thirty days. Also, if you decide you don't want your cat any longer, you may have to promise to return it to the shelter rather than give it to another owner or let it run loose.

To find out more, you should check your local animal shelter or write Adopt-a-Cat Month Information Desk, Suite 1300, 211 East Ontario, Chicago, Illinois 60611.

But shelters are not the only route to cat ownership. What about prospective owners who think they may want a pedigreed feline?

For Those Who Prefer a Pedigree

Some people feel it's important to know the mother, father, and other genealogical roots of their pet. In other words, they are inclined to find a cat with a pedigree.

If you're in this category, be prepared to pay for it. A kitten with a pedigree, especially one who has some cat-show grand champions in her background, can cost hundreds of dollars. The cost of the animal is determined by the breed, bloodlines, type, and markings.

Basically there are three types of cats you can purchase from a breeder:

- *A show-quality cat.* This cat should become a top show cat and may cost $1,000 to $2,000 or more, and depends on the breed, bloodlines, type, and markings.
- *A breeder-quality cat.* Because of his genetic background, this cat is a good candidate to produce winning offspring for cat shows. The cost of these breeders begins at four hundred dollars.
- *A pet-quality cat.* Although not qualified to be in the show ring or to become a grand champion, many pet-quality cats may have a pedigree and can make great companions because their temperament is known. The price of these beautiful animals begins at around $100.

To find a cat with a pedigree, you can try several routes to ownership:

- A local cat show, sponsored by The Cat Fanciers' Association, American Cat Fanciers' Association, The International Cat Association, or in Canada the Canadian Cat Association. Owners and breeders showing and attending will be able to help you out.

- Listings in legitimate cat magazines or publications, such as *Cats Magazine, Cat Fancy Magazine, I Love Cats* magazine, or the *Cat Fancy Almanac.*
- Listings from the Cat Fanciers' Association. Just write or call the central office at P.O. Box 1005, Manasquan, New Jersey 08736-0805. Telephone: (908) 528-9797.
- A local veterinarian. Many "animal doctors" can refer you to a good breeder.

The breeder should be willing to provide you with a written pedigree. Also, you should ask for a health guarantee from the seller and be sure to secure an agreement that your veterinarian will check out the cat before the sale becomes final.

Some typical "cat contracts" accompany this text. The clauses in these form agreements are simply suggestions, and they may be weighed too heavily in favor of the seller. You should feel free to modify them, and I'd suggest that you hire a lawyer for this purpose. Some of the points in these forms may be illegal in some states, and special considerations in a particular sale may require special contractual provisions.

How to Cross-examine a Cat Breeder

You should *not* be lulled into complacency just because a cat you're considering has a pedigree. The points about health and liveliness that I listed in the discussion of shelter cats also apply to cats with an established lineage.

Conditional Sales Agreement

Kitten Born _____
Name _____
Description _____
Sire _____
Dam _____
Show Approval _____
Purchase Price _____

The above kitten is sold to _____
on _____ with the understand that he / she is not
to be used for breeding purposes. The kitten must be cas-
trated / spayed between 6 and 9 months of age.

Upon receipt of a licensed veterinarian's written certification,
showing that an altering operation has been performed, the
above kitten's pedigree and registration application will be
forwarded if requested. If altering certification has not been
received by _____, the undersigned
Buyer agrees that the Breeder has the right to reclaim the
above kitten without refund of the purchase price. Reasonable
legal fees incurred in so doing will be paid by the Buyer.

Medical Record   Signed _____
                              Buyer

                              _____
                              _____

                              Address

                              _____
                              Telephone

                              _____
                              Breeder

SOURCE: Cat Fanciers' Association.

Cat or Kitten Contract

Breed _____ Color _____ Sex _____
Name (if applicable) _____
Birth Date _____ Litter Reg # or Reg # _____
Sire _____
Dam _____
Sold to _____ Telephone _____
Address _____
Sold to _____ Telephone _____
For the following price or terms _____
_____ Date Paid _____

PURCHASER AGREES TO THE FOLLOWING:

1. Under no circumstances will this cat or kitten be sold, leased or given away, or sold to any pet shop, research laboratory or similar facility.

2. This cat or kitten will be kept indoors and not be allowed to roam freely outside.

3. This cat or kitten is purchased for Pet _____ Breeding _____ Show _____

4. If purchased as a pet, Purchaser agrees to castrate or spay this cat between the ages of 6 months and 1 year, or within 30 days after purhase if this is an adult cat, and agrees and guarantees that this cat or kitten WILL NOT be used for stud or breeding.

5. If this cat or kitten is found to be neglected or mistreated, Purchaser will surrender said cat or kitten to Seller, unconditionally.

6. Seller agrees to provide pedigree and registration papers for this cat or kitten upon presentation of a veterinarian's certificate of castrating or spaying. Yes _____ No _____

(continued)

(continued from previous page)

7. This cat or kitten cannot be shown without written permission of the Seller.

8. No cash refunds.

9. If this cat is purchased as a breeder male, Purchaser agrees not to use this cat for outside stud service, except as follows: _____

_____

10. If this cat is purchased as a breeder male, Purchaser agrees not to resell the cat for stud to anyone unless approved by the Seller.

11. Vaccinated _____

Vaccine used _____ Needs revaccination _____

12. Purchaser has three working days to have blood test on this cat or kitten for feline leukemia virus.

13. Seller makes no guarantees as to the health or show quality of this cat or kitten, except as follows: _____

_____

14. This cat or kitten is being fed _____

15. Other conditions of sale are as follows: _____

_____

_____

Purchaser's signature indicates full agreement of all above conditions.

Signature of Purchaser _____ Date_____

Signature of Seller _____ Date_____

SOURCE: Cat Fanciers' Association.

It's also important to look at the breeder's physical setting and overall operation with a critical eye. Here are some pertinent questions you might ask:

- Are his facilities clean and neat?
- Do his cats look healthy and well cared for?

As a general rule a breeder won't allow you to go into his "cattery" to see the cats, but you might ask anyhow.

- Is he showing his own cats? Are his cats winning? If so, that could indicate that he is maintaining a well-run operation.
- Does he have any grand champions in his background? If he does, that indicates that his methods have resulted in considerable success.
- What references can he provide to put you in touch with others who have bought cats from him? A breeder should be happy to give you these references if he has been pleasing his customers. Typically a good breeder will establish lasting friendships with buyers of his cats. But if he *won't* give you references, find another breeder.
- Is he a member of a cat breeders association? He should be.
- Is he a certified judge for cat competitions? If he is, rest assured that this breeder takes good care of his or her cats.
- Finally, does he really seem to know what he's doing? Can he answer your questions with confidence? It's important to use your common sense in evaluating a breeder, even if you don't understand every aspect of his work.

Answering these and similar questions will give you a clue as to the quality of breeder, as well as the quality of cat he is selling and you are buying.

And Now It's the Breeder's Turn

Don't be surprised if, after you're through asking your questions, the breeder begins to grill *you*. You can get some idea of his concerns from the clauses in the cat-contract forms. He'll want to check you out to make sure that the cat he sells you will have a good, loving home.

Here are some possible issues he may raise with you:

- Do you have other cats, dogs, or pets in the house? If so, have you made provision for the new cat to fit in well and be safe?
- Where *exactly* will the cat live in your home?
- What type of work hours do you have? If you're away a lot, a cat that needs considerable companionship may not be for you.
- Do you have any references? The breeder may want *you* to demonstrate that you have a good track record with pets.
- Will the cat be allowed to go outdoors? A breeder simply won't sell you a cat that will have to spend much time outdoors.
- Is the cat going to be a pet, a breeder, or a show animal?

This last question is important in that the answer will influence the price of your cat. As you already know, show cats cost a great deal more than pets.

Also, if you plan to keep the cat only as a pet, you'll have to guarantee that you'll have it spayed or neutered within thirty days.

All this detail and these back-and-forth inquiries may seem an enormous amount of work for the purchase of a cat. But when a pedigree animal is involved, the procedure is par for the course. Breeders care deeply about the cats they breed and the homes where those cats end up living out their lives.

Also, even if you shell out a couple of thousand dollars for a show cat, you may reap a many-fold return on your investment. The grand champion for 1990 was sold for $15,000!

In addition, when the sale has been completed, the breeder may well become your greatest unpaid resource and consultant. Because he cares so much about his animals, he'll probably be willing to give you many cat-care tips.

Finally the breeder's questions will help *you* in finding the right cat for your lifestyle. It is important that the cat be happy with you, but also that you be happy with the cat!

What Kind of Cat?

What are some of the types of pedigree cats you might buy? Although there are too many breeds for me to describe them all, here are a few you may want to consider, along with some general personality traits that owners and breeders have noted.

American Shorthair   This cat is known as a "work-ing breed" because it gained its reputation as a barn cat, chasing mice and other pests. The American genealogy of this cat is more ancient than that of many humans: This cat first arrived on our shores with the Pilgrims and other European settlers.

With a square, well-defined muzzle, and easy-to-groom coat, the Shorthair comes in thirty-four different colors, has a pleasant temperament, and can be a good pet for children.

American shorthair   LARRY JOHNSON   Copyright © 1992

Abyssinian   This breed has sometimes been called a "dog lover's cat" because it is often very friendly and playful, like a puppy. The breed originated in Egypt as a temple cat and has been bred in recent times to look like the old temple cats. In fact the modern variation has been interbred with wild cats to maintain the clean, sleek body type.

A medium-sized cat, the Abyssinian typically has short hair, a modified wedge-shaped face, and almond-shaped eyes. He's too active to sit in your lap for long periods, but he prefers to be in company and will play endlessly with you and another cat.

Abyssinian   LARRY JOHNSON   Copyright © 1992

Somali   This cat, which comes in gold and red variations, is a longhaired Abyssinian. They are characterized by a clarity in color of their coat, modified wedge-shaped face without flat planes, and almond-shaped eyes. Their temperament is similar to that of other Abyssinians.

Somali   LARRY JOHNSON   Copyright © 1992

Siamese   This regal, mysterious-looking cat has short hair and a playful personality. The pointed ears, glistening coat, and distinctive dark tail, legs, and facial markings practically scream out, "I have a pedigree!"

Siamese   LARRY JOHNSON   Copyright © 1992

Persian   There are many types of Persians, such as the Himalayan. This breed has the Persian's distinctive long hair, flat face, and placid temperament.

Persian   LARRY JOHNSON   Copyright © 1992

British Shorthair   This breed is typically British—quiet, understated, "laid back." The cat tends to be quite stout, full-cheeked, and some say "Churchillian-looking." The British Shorthair is noted for a beautiful, dense coat, large head, and large, prominent eyes. Like the American Shorthair, this cat is a "working breed," in that it will chase mice or any other small creatures that invade your home.

British shorthair   LARRY JOHNSON   Copyright © 1992

Russian Blue   This small, slender cat, which came from a port in Russia to England in 1900, is characterized by a silver-blue coat, flared ears, and emerald-green eyes. There is a suggestion of Siamese in the Blue, mainly because the Siamese was cross-bred with it in the early days to save the Russian Blue breed. These tend to be one-person cats who are a little shy and don't mind being alone.

Russian blue   LARRY JOHNSON   Copyright © 1992

Sphinx   This hairless cat is a very rare breed. There's a little fur on the face, ears, feet, and tail, but the rest of the body is coated by down or "peach fuzz"—a major advantage to those who are allergic to cat hair. This highly muscled cat has a solid, rubbery, suedelike feel.

Sphinx   LARRY JOHNSON
Copyright © 1992

Javanese   With a long, tapered body, long hair, and long, fluffy tail, this cat is fine-boned, yet muscular. As a pet, it's usually good with children because of its mellow personality.

Javanese   LARRY JOHNSON   Copyright © 1992

Exotic Shorthair   The easygoing temperament of this cat may remind you of a Persian, but it's much easier to groom. In fact the cat is known as a shorthair Persian or a lazy man's Persian because it's the product of a union between an American Shorthair and a Persian.

Exotic shorthair
LARRY JOHNSON   Copyright
© 1992

Ocicat   There are several breeds of "Ossie," including the Tawny and the Chocolate Spotted. This breed is a result of crossing an Abyssinian with a Siamese. Ocicats can grow quite large, fourteen to sixteen pounds, but they can also be wonderful playmates and good household cats. The Ossie will often meet strangers at the door, roll balls about, and fetch things that are thrown. This cat has a close, shiny coat, a heavy, powerful neck and head, and an indentation in the nose. In many ways the Ossie has a wild look, though it's wholly domesticated. It's people-oriented, likes to travel, and usually gets along well with other cats.

Ocicat   LARRY JOHNSON   Copyright © 1992

Havana Brown   This breed is small and slender and was derived in the 1950s by crossing a chocolate-colored Siamese with a black cat. The Brown has a lightbulb-shaped head, emerald-green eyes, and a rather large, exaggerated muzzle. This cat is very people-oriented and doglike. Many Browns have been trained to retrieve, and they love human companionship.

Havana brown   LARRY JOHNSON   Copyright © 1992

Burman, or Sacred Cat of Burma   This breed originated in Thailand, moved to France, and finally made it to the United States in the early 1960s. These cats have sapphire-blue eyes, white feet, bell-shaped ears, a Roman nose, and a long body with a fluffy coat. It's been said that these cats "never seem to grow up. They constantly act like fun-loving kittens."

Burman   LARRY JOHNSON
Copyright © 1992

Devon Rex   Major characteristics of this breed are a short, pixy-shaped head, large ears, and a reasonably elegant coat. They were identified in Devonshire, England, in 1960 after a cat that was abandoned in a tin mine was mated with a Cornish Rex. These cats don't like to be left alone. They prefer human company constantly and are willing to fetch and perform other tricks.

Devon rex   LARRY JOHNSON   Copyright © 1992

Bombay   This black cat was created by a Louisville, Kentucky, woman who mated a black American Shorthair with a sable Burmese. The Bombay has a short, chunky body, copper eyes, and a black, shiny coat that clings close to the body. He also has a broad chest, rounded head, and considerable physical strength. These make good pets, either with other cats or in a one-cat household.

Bombay   LARRY JOHNSON   Copyright © 1992

Scottish Fold   This cat has unusual small, stubby ears that seem to be folded over, back against the skull—hence the name of the breed. They were first recognized as a separate breed in the United States in 1974, and they have since gained a reputation as good pets who love human company.

Scottish fold   LARRY JOHNSON   Copyright © 1992

Japanese Bobtail   This black-and-white cat is an ancient breed from Japan. Originally a street cat, it was brought over to this country by members of the U.S. military. Though fun-loving and lively, this cat isn't as playful as the Abyssinian. The triangular-shaped face, large ears, cored-up nose, medium-short coat, and curved, pom-pomlike tail give it a distinctive appearance in the cat-show scene.

Japanese bobtail
LARRY JOHNSON   Copyright
© 1992

Maine Coon   The largest of the domesticated cats, the Maine Coon is a native of North America and has made its mark as a working cat—or mouse chaser—in the New England states. With a thick, shaggy coat, broad chest, and long body, the Maine Coon has a marvelous disposition and has been called "the gentle giant."

Maine coon   LARRY JOHNSON   Copyright © 1992

Manx   The four kinds of Manx cat are known for one major feature—the lack of a tail. This stocky cat comes in many different colors and has large eyes, massive bones, and a sweet temperament. While some other cats may seem drowsy or languid, this one always appears alert.

Manx   LARRY JOHNSON   Copyright © 1992

Chartreux   The origins of this beautiful French breed have been lost in history, though records do date back to the sixteenth century in the network of French monasteries. These cats have big, round, wide-set eyes and tend to be silent—reportedly because their ancestors took a vow of silence in the monasteries where they once lived! Both males and females have full coats, though the males' are plusher.

Chartreux   LARRY JOHNSON   Copyright © 1

Norwegian Forest Cat   This rare breed has a triangular head, heavy bones, slanted eyes, a straight nose, a broad muzzle, powerful legs and feet, and a full, water-repellent coat. The cat is affectionate and people-oriented.

Norwegian forest cat
LARRY JOHNSON   Copyright
© 1992

Obviously, there are many more pedigreed cats that we could talk about, but these descriptions should give you a good general idea about the traits of some of the most popular breeds.

Whatever kind of cat you choose, however—whether a shelter cat or a feline with a pedigree—the transition from the old home to your home must be smooth. Also, if you have the available space, consider having two cats instead of just one. This will give your cat a playmate of his own size, and make him far happier than being alone. In the next chapter we'll explore some standard, proven steps to help your new pet adjust well to the new environment

CHAPTER THREE

GETTING YOUR NEW PET OFF ON THE RIGHT PAW

Making a choice of a pet cat is only the first small step in a successful and rewarding relationship. When you take that animal through your front door, you begin the experience of *living* with him—and that can be quite a challenging task, even if you do some intelligent prior planning.

In many ways getting ready for a new cat is like getting ready for a new child. In fact I've encountered many cat owners who treat their pets as one of the family, an attitude that nonowners find a bit eccentric but that seasoned cat owners know can be quite healthy. Those who have a warm, loving view toward their pets are more likely to include their animal in their daily routine, treat them well, avoid abuse, and provide them with appropriate training and medical services.

To help you get that new cat settled in your home, there are several initial questions that you should ask yourself as a new owner, or as an individual who already owns pets:

- Do I have adequate time to devote to a cat?
- How many cats should I own?
- What should I name my cat?
- How should I introduce my cat to my other pets?
- How should I introduce the cat to other family members?
- Are there any special things I need to know about my cat's first visit to the vet?
- Can I afford to own a cat?

Before you bring a cat into your household, you should ask yourself each of these questions. Some thoughts follow about the best way to answer some of these queries.

QUESTION 1
Do I Have Adequate Time to Devote to a Cat?

It's no secret that the cat has become the most popular pet in America. The reasons are simple: Cats are relatively care-free, in the sense that they don't require much of an owner's time. They don't need to be walked; they keep themselves clean; they usually don't eat more than they need; and they can be cuddly and friendly in varying degrees, depending on the breed.

Even with these undemanding traits, however, your cat will need some quality time with you. If you travel a great deal, you shouldn't own a cat—or any other animal, for that matter. If your budget is very tight, having a pet may not be advisable because keeping a cat does cost money. You'll have to purchase cat food, pay for vet visits, cover the cost of annual shots, buy kitty litter, and provide cat toys. None of these basic responsibilities cover emergencies such as a broken leg, runny eyes, or other illness that may require your attention at home.

Also, even though a cat can easily entertain himself, he still needs some interaction with you. Simple games such as rolling a ball, dangling a string with a small piece of cloth tied to it, or otherwise playing with the pet takes time and attention. So be aware of some of the basic duties of ownership before you make your final decision!

QUESTION 2
How Many Cats Should I Own?

The city fathers in Syracuse, New York, recently became concerned because stray cats seemed to be breeding on the streets at an alarming rate. They proposed passing a local law prohibiting citizens from having more than three cats or dogs. When the general public learned of the plan, the claws of the cat-owning public were bared. A massive pro-feline lobby emerged with a public relations campaign consisting of letters and phone calls to local legislators and a rash of communications to the press. The end result: The proposal was put on indefinite hold, and cat lovers were left with the freedom to have two cats or twenty—or as many more as they wished.

Although some other cities, such as Milwaukee, have succeeded in restricting the number of pets that one family can own, I'm generally against such rules. There are enough strays around, as well as needy animals in shelters, that I feel those with the capacity to house extra pets should be allowed that option.

On the other hand, I think it's wise for most people to bring home *only one cat at a time*. The main reason is that, like people, every cat has her own personality. Consequently with each cat you'll have to make special adjustments in getting her settled, introducing her to other pets and family members. You will have to spend some time helping her feel comfortable and become adapted to her new surroundings in your household. Taking in two cats at the same time will make this process doubly difficult. Three cats triples your responsibilities. If you are unable to devote the time or energy to doing a good job in the first days and weeks of adjustment, you, your cat, and the rest of your household will suffer in the long run for the neglect.

As time-consuming as having more than one cat may sound, you should still seriously consider the two-cat option. With two cats you'll not only get double the enjoyment, but you'll also give each cat a playmate. By providing a companion that each can chase, tease, and sleep with, you'll reduce dramatically the loneliness factor that may plague a single cat, even if that cat is in a very attending household.

If you do decide to get more than one cat, try to find animals that are around the same age. Many cat owners make the mistake of purchasing a baby kitten for their older cat with the idea that the young one will perk up the older. That's like giving an infant to a human who is in his eighties or nineties!

Note: Even as you decide on the number of pets you want, keep in mind my basic advice about birth control: Every cat or dog you own should be spayed or neutered.

QUESTION 3
What Should I Name My Cat?

Many people become stymied when they acquire a new cat because they somehow can't seem to find the right name. Again, it's similar to having a child. The name you choose is going to be with that child all his life.

Those with a specially bred cat, which has a pedigree, may feel compelled to call their cat something majestic, such as Sir Percival IV, or Lady Highborn. That approach is fine and may go over very well in the tough, competitive atmosphere of cat shows.

As for me, I'm more inclined to the whimsical or quirky. I had one cat that I named Peaches because I got her in the state of Georgia. So it's understandable that I was quite taken with the story of one cat named For Sale.

For Sale   Joe was looking for a roommate, and so he placed an ad in the newspaper. After several interviews he finally found a fellow named Al, who seemed compatible. The only hitch was that Al had two pure-bred Siamese kittens.

Now, Joe liked cats all right, but he thought the apartment was too small for two men *and* two pets. So they agreed that Al could bring in his two kittens on a *temporary* basis. Al would have to find both of them a new home as soon as possible.

All went well with the first kitten. He quickly charmed a new owner and was out of the apartment in no time. But things went much more slowly with the second animal. Al placed ad after ad in the paper, with the heading FOR SALE, but there were no takers. After a few weeks the two men realized that they might have a third permanent resident on their hands, and it was only appropriate that they give him a name. The best option seemed to be For Sale, since that had been his status for so long.

But the story doesn't end here.

Apparently For Sale was influenced by the lifestyle of his two bachelor roommates. He became quite the cat-about-town as he roamed about the neighborhood, making liaisons with all the available female cats. Also, For Sale developed a real macho, aggressive personality, in part because his owners played constantly and roughhoused with him. They even taught him to heel, fetch, and do other doglike tricks.

On one occasion For Sale was missing for several days, and Joe and Al combed the surrounding neighborhoods for him. As they searched, they learned that many of the neighbors were unhappy with their tomcat because he had developed a reputation for having multiple girlfriends and screaming at the top of his lungs in the middle of the night. Days later, when Joe and Al were sitting around their apartment, they heard a scratch at a window. Joe looked out, and there was For Sale, exhausted and somewhat dirty from his tomcatting, but otherwise looking all right. Joe ushered the wayward pet to his accustomed cat corner, where he fell dead asleep for hours.

For Sale's escapades finally got completely out of hand, and his life was changed for good. He used to hang out under the porch of an elderly woman who owned a female cat. Each time the woman came home from shopping, she would fumble with the door, and For Sale learned to take advantage of the situation: He would jump out from under her porch, run through the door into the house, and chase the female cat. The woman would become so exasperated that she would try to beat For Sale off with a broom. Not to be put off in the heat of his passion, For Sale once attacked the woman. Fortunately no one was hurt, but the woman did call the local authorities to have the cat picked

Actress Joan Van Ark and her cat

up. Joe and Al were soon notified, and they were given an ultimatum: Have For Sale altered or lose him forever! Now in his new neutered state, For Sale is a much calmer and more obedient cat.

A word or phrase that's reminiscent of a warm or meaningful past experience or place can also be appropriate to inspire the naming of a cat. That was the case with Joan Van Ark, star of the television series *Knots Landing*.

The Naming of Snug Harbor   "I hope my other cats don't ever read this, but Snug is my favorite—Snug Harbor, to be exact. It's always been that way—ever since I first laid eyes on him at the Snug Harbor Tavern in Lincoln City, Oregon.

"We were up there shooting *Knots,* and my husband told me there was a mother cat with five of the cutest kittens that I just *had* to see. I walked in, and sure enough, there was a big black-and-white 'mommy' with five kittens, seriously nursing away, having dinner. One—the *only* black-and-white kitten—pulled away momentarily and looked up at me, mustache and all. It was love at first sight. Snug Harbor went home with me in my lap on the plane."

Certainly this cat has developed his own personality and has contributed over the years to Joan's happiness in ways that have nothing to do with Snug Harbor. But the name itself has a certain degree of power. It periodically conjures up a compelling, distant memory of Oregon—a warm experience of the past that will forever be linked to one little black-and-white kitten.

QUESTION 4
How Should I Introduce My Cat to My Other Pets?

Many times animal lovers have more than one pet—and that can create some complications for the "new cat on the block." Here are some guidelines if you're in this situation.

Controlling the First Encounter   Before you physically carry your new cat through the door of your home, introduce it briefly to your pet in the following way:

In separate cars take the new cat and your old pet to an area that's new to both animals. Carefully allow the pets to interact with each other. Physical contact should be limited to prevent the transmission of any diseases, parasites, or other health conditions. One family member can hold, pet, or softly speak to each animal. Once the animals are somewhat familiar with each other—and have done a little mutual sniffing—take them back home together in the same car. In human terms the old pet who goes through this procedure has welcomed the new pet into the household. In effect he's allowed the newcomer to enter his home.

As strange as this approach may seem, people who have taken the time to follow it have seen an almost instant friendship develop between the animals. This sort of encounter is nonthreatening to the old pet because he won't feel as though he's being deserted by his owner. At the same time the new cat feels welcomed. Once the new animal is in the home, you move on to the quarantine phase.

The Quarantine   The next principle is to quarantine the new pet for two weeks, just to be sure that he doesn't have a health problem. Contagious diseases or parasites could be present and might infect your old pet, so you want to do all you can to stop the spread of any illness before it gets started.

Having the new cat in the house but not in direct contact with your other cat for this two-week period has another benefit: You'll give them both an opportunity to get used to each other's presence—at a safe distance. If there's a door between them, they can sniff at one another through the crack without having to deal with a face-to-face meeting.

Supervising Later Encounters   When the two cats finally do get together, it's a *must* to supervise their first few encounters. Also, allow the older cat to have a place to which he can retreat, outside the presence of the new cat. For example, you might set aside one room where only the old cat is allowed and then shut the door after he enters.

You'll most likely find that the new cat won't use the litter box of the old cat because the first cat will have "marked" it. That is, the smells and other signs of use will cause the new cat to look elsewhere, for his *own* bathroom. So it will be necessary to set up a second, separate litter box for the new cat. Cats are territorial creatures who quickly stake out a claim to their surroundings. If another pet is already there, some amount of conflict will be almost inevitable—especially if a dog is involved.

If you already have a dog in the house, the interaction between the new cat and the dog should always be supervised closely during the first few meetings. The first encounter is quite likely to be a shock on both sides. If you're there to smooth things over, the relationship will have a better chance of getting off on the right foot.

In many cases, however, the dog and cat simply won't ever become friends. They may tolerate each other when you're around, but when you leave, fights or chases may break out. For this reason it's important always to provide a cat with some kind of escape route, such as a sturdy high bookcase shelf, where she can quickly get out of the dog's reach. Some dogs are natural-born "catters," who could easily injure or kill an unwary new kitten.

The byword for introducing a new cat into an environment where there are other animals is *slowly*. The cat must be moved gradually into the household. Whenever possible, he should be the one to take the first step in making friends or otherwise becoming socialized.

Like every other dog and cat, Scruffette and Crudge had an adjustment period to go through and I was concerned. However, now they are like old buddies—playing, chasing one another down the hall, and following me around the house. When I work, they both lie down about a foot away from one another and sleep. Proof! Cats and dogs *can* get along—eventually.

QUESTION 5
How Should I Introduce the Cat to Other Family Members?

You may notice that a cat seems to have a sixth sense that enables him to home in on a person who doesn't like him or doesn't want him around. More often than not, the cat will go right over to that individual, even though there may be plenty of others who are trying to pet him or get him into their laps.

Why the perverse pleasure in showing attention to the unfriendly human? I really don't think cats are perverse or masochistic; rather, they probably head for the unfriendly person because while everyone else is milling about, gesticulating, trying to woo the cat, the cat hater is trying to make himself inconspicuous. He sits there quietly, afraid to move a muscle for fear that this might be interpreted by the cat as a come-on or as friendliness. But the strategy backfires because most cats *prefer* a minimum of motion and a quiet lap! The moral is simple: If you *don't* want a cat to bother you, appear gregarious, gesture wildly, or beg him to come over. Say, "Here, kitty, kitty!" as passionately as possible. The chances are the cat will keep his distance . . . maybe!

On the other hand, if you *do* desperately want a cat to favor you, just sit motionless in your seat. In fact you might try looking the other way. Most likely that cat will be in your lap in an instant!

These observations have a direct application for humans who are having their first series of encounters with a new cat. It's best for everyone to let the cat make the first overtures. People who try to push themselves on the kitten will probably drive him away—and may get scratched.

This approach has a special application to children, who often develop a relationship with their cats that is quite different from that with their dogs. Although dogs frequently develop simple, straightforward friendships with the kids in their household, cats can be much more complex.

I'm reminded of a story of a cat named Gypsy, owned by Judy Peizer, who writes for television. Gypsy loved the children in her neighborhood, but also wanted to exercise considerable control over them. The toddlers and preschoolers played in a wooded area that adjoined several houses, and Gypsy would cavort around among the trees and bushes with the little boys and girls.

But there was a catch to the friendship. Whenever possible, Gypsy would take their gloves, mittens, or other belongings and transport them over to her own yard. Then, when the children tried to retrieve their things, she would block their way when they tried to go back to their own homes. In other words, she enjoyed "herding" the kids in the area onto her own turf, like so many human cattle, and trapping them there!

The mothers of these youngsters finally complained so loudly that Gypsy had to be brought permanently indoors.

But by the last report I had, she still follows their every move intently through an open window. And I'm sure, given the slightest opening, she would return to her old child-herding ways at full throttle!

If you have children in your home, give them this advice about the new cat:

- Approach the cat from a sitting position, which will make you appear smaller. As far as your cat is concerned, you look like a giant.
- Be gentle toward the cat.
- Respect her privacy and her need to take the initiative in relationships.
- Avoid too much excitement when you're relating to your cat. Dogs often like jumping around, shouting, and laughing, but cats usually don't. They like to play, but they also prefer people in their presence to be relatively quiet, or at least more subdued than most dog lovers.
- Leave the cat alone when she's tired. Kittens are babies and need to spend much of the day resting, and if anyone upsets them when they are fatigued or sleepy, they may lash out. Keep in mind that the average cat sleeps eighteen hours a day!
- Take time to play with your cat every day. There are many simple games that require only a little of your time, but can give your cat the exercise and attention he needs. We'll talk about those games in the chapter "The Aerobic Cat."
- Be sensitive when your cat has been handled too

much. She will squirm and try to get away from you. Don't try to force her to stay.
- Leave the cat (and all other pets) alone completely when she's eating. *Never* tease an animal when he's eating. If you do, you'll probably end up causing undesirable, aggressive behavior in the pet especially during mealtime.

Children should also be taught to wash their hands thoroughly after they have finished playing with a cat. And if they are scratched or bitten, the wound should be immediately washed out, antiseptic should be applied, and a clean bandage should be used to cover it. Cat bites and scratches become infected more often than those from any other pet, so children or adults who have been injured should watch the wound for spreading redness, pain, or any other signs of infection.

QUESTION 6
When Should I First Take My Cat to the Vet?

Usually your kitten's first visit to the veterinarian should occur when the animal is about six to eight weeks old. It's best for the kitten to stay close to the mother until it is weaned at about six weeks. After that a thorough medical exam is in order to identify any diseases or parasites and to begin the required round of vaccinations.

On the first visit the vet will perform a complete checkup, including an examination of the animal's stool to see if there are any parasites or worms, so you'll have to take a stool sample to the vet's office. Also, he will probably perform a leukemia test. The vet will pay particular attention to the cat's general appearance, including the following indications of good health:

- A reasonable level of friskiness or physical activity without being aggressive
- A shiny coat
- The presence of a purring response when the cat is touched
- The absence of sneezing or other outward signs or symptoms of illness

At six to eight weeks the vet will also begin a series of vaccinations that will be completed when the cat is about four months of age. Annual boosters will follow in subsequent years.

These include shots for distemper, rabies, and various respiratory viruses. It's *essential* for all cats, even those who spend all their time indoors, to have these shots, and especially the rabies vaccinations. Infection can occur if the cat gets out of the house just once or if he comes into contact with another diseased animal in his own home.

A Note on Spaying, Neutering, and Declawing

As I mentioned in the previous chapter, you should have your female cat spayed (i.e., have the ovaries removed) and your male cat neutered (have the testes removed). One of the biggest problems we now face is an overpopulation of cats, many of whom are strays who briefly live and then die in shelters because they can't find homes.

Ultimately many of those in the streets will acquire contagious diseases or otherwise become nuisances. Tomcats tend to roam about, get into fights with other cats, and are at a higher risk for various medical problems, such as leukemia and abscesses. The cats who remain in shelters usually become the victims of euthanasia, simply because our society lacks the facilities, homes, or means to support them. The best solution is birth control through spaying and neutering.

These procedures should be performed by the vet at about six months of age for both males and females. Sometimes, though, owners prefer to wait two to three months longer for the males so that they can develop certain masculine characteristics.

If you are having a difficult time deciding whether or not to spay or neuter your cat—perhaps because you may think you want it to have kittens—please remember the following points:

- Many shelters have to kill up to three hundred animals a weekend because no one wants them.
- If your cat is spayed or neutered, you'll never have to lose sleep worrying about whether or not your cat's offspring are meeting an early death in an animal shelter because an owner for them couldn't be found.

What might happen if you *don't* have your cat altered? Cats have minds of their own. They don't like to take direction, whether the command comes from the TV director or the cat's owner. Here's an adventurous account by our producer, Jamie Maury: "I recall one particular feline encounter that remains a painful memory for the TV crew. We were videotaping cat health segments with a veterinarian and a large tomcat. As soon as the vet started talking about the importance of spay and neuter, the well-endowed tom took off. Several brave TV crew members fell victim to scratch attacks from this aggressive tom, who refused to be removed from the cozy confines of the television backdrop. Needless to say, the cat remained in his secluded corner for the duration of the taping day.

"This on-camera catastrophe abated when we replaced the missing tomcat with a neutered Persian, who dozed under the warm studio lights. Finally, at the end of the day, the tomcat emerged from his hiding spot to check out some young female felines that had arrived in the studio. Distracted by his interest in the other cats, the tomcat was apprehended and placed in his kitty crate. And so ends yet another cat tale about tension among unaltered felines and trying to feature cats on camera."

Declawing   As for declawing, I have just one word: *Don't!* The declawing operation is very painful—somewhat comparable to a human's having his fingernails pulled out. Some vets will condone declawing so long as the operation is performed only on the front paws. I'd recommend that you spare your pet this excruciating procedure under any circumstances.

If you do decide to declaw your cat, be prepared for the worst. You'll have to watch him limp around in pain for days and look at you with very sad eyes. A close friend of mine said that declawing her cat was one of the most terrible decisions of her life. It broke her heart to watch the pain and suffering she and her husband had caused the pet.

There's another consideration that argues against declawing: If your cat spends any time outdoors, or if he escapes outside just once in his life, a lack of claws could mean your cat's life. Not only will he be unable to defend himself if a hostile dog or cat should appear on the scene, but because cats are natural climbers, he could suffer a damaging fall if he tries to go up into a tree or onto other high places in your neighborhood.

An Introduction to Some Antidotes to Cat Clawing

Cats like to scratch away at everything when they are young, but as they grow older, they tend to settle down. Yet even during their most active ripping-and-tearing period, there are several ways to minimize the damage. A friendly, well-aimed shot of a squirt gun, for instance, will keep him off your furniture or other places where he doesn't belong.

Also, as Dr. Michael Fox, the syndicated columnist and renowned animal-book author, has told me, it helps to place a little catnip on areas that are "on limits" for your cat. For example, you might rub some on a scratching post or an old piece of carpet. The catnip will attract the cat, and he'll learn that these places will allow him complete freedom to stretch, scratch, and bare his claws.

If you make a scratching post for your cat, be sure that it's sturdy and taller than your cat when he is in a stretched position. He'll want to stretch his muscles and limbs on it much as you like to stretch when you get up in the morning.

CHAPTER FOUR

CHARACTER-ISTICS OF A CARING OWNER

SOMEBODY ONCE SAID that true love is measured by what you do for others, not just by what you say. In this vein there are four absolutely essential actions that show whether a person *really* loves his cat: grooming, feeding, litter tending, and spending time with the pet.

Good grooming reflects a concern by the owner that the cat feels good, looks good, and relates well to the outside world. Nutritious feeding may be the most important preventive measure to ensure that the pet stays healthy. And taking care of the litter box demonstrates that the owner cares enough to get down on hands and knees and serve a feline friend who needs some help maintaining a clean "bathroom." The time spent in performing these services will ensure a happy and healthy pet, and take very little time for the owner.

Is Your Cat Well Groomed?

It's easy to tell whether your cat is well groomed. The three key points that show a particular cat is "dressed for success" through proper grooming are claws, fur, and a lack of fleas.

But even though you may accept these points, your cat may want to fight you at every step of the grooming process. So at the outset your attitude toward grooming must be rooted in three *additional* points: patience, patience, and more patience.

CLAWS

Claws are the first things anyone will notice, perhaps because they are the first things that scratch the skin or rip the clothing. And that doesn't make a very good impression on any cat owner or visitor, even one who is a chronic cat lover!

As I've already said, I don't believe that any cat should be declawed. The operation that removes the claws of these pets is both painful and dangerous. If a cat without claws goes outdoors and either tries to climb or defend himself, he could be seriously hurt or even killed. But if you follow this advice and let your cat keep those claws, how do you protect yourself, your furniture, and your guests?

The answer: The claws must be clipped on a regular basis. When I've mentioned this to some new owners, they blanch and say, "She'll never hold still for that! I'll be shredded! Gale, you're nuts!"

It's true that if you use the wrong technique for clipping, you may be shredded. Cats don't like to be restrained. Try to keep any cat immobile for even a couple of seconds, and she'll begin to struggle, often violently. Also, cats are particularly sensitive about having their paws held against their will. A tip on holding a cat is that you

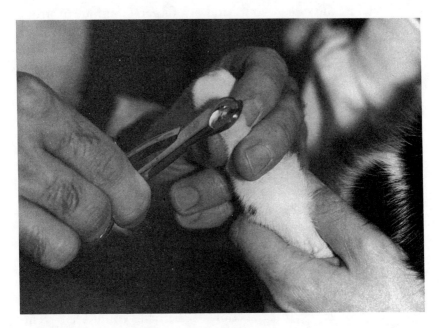

Clipping a cat's toenails. Gently press the paw to extend the claws so you can see the claw.   MIKE POTTER   Copyright © 1992

should try to cuddle and support him from the rear or underneath, but *never* just grab his paws and try to clip the claws.

So how do you clip claws without holding onto paws? Remember the first grooming rule, *be patient!* And the second rule is, *take your time.* In the beginning, clipping claws and basic grooming may be frustrating, but with time these duties will be done more easily. Eventually they will become a time that you actually enjoy sharing with your cat.

The best approach to clipping is to place the cat in your lap and simply rub his head and stroke him. Make the pet feel comfortable. Establish a trusting relationship. Then, after the cat is comfortable, you can begin with the first claw.

Allow the cat to support himself with his paws resting

against the side of your hand or a finger. Continue to stroke him so that he is resting easily in your arms. Next, push gently with a finger against the base of the claw you want to cut, and the claw will jut out. Cat claws are retractable, and you can make them stick out by applying this type of gentle pressure.

Then, using special blunt cat-nail clippers that you can buy in most pet stores, or at cat shows, insert the end of the nail into blades, just below the large part of the nail. Cat claws have two parts: a thin, sharp section at the very end which culminates in a point; and a thick section closer to the paw. You can usually see the blood line in the thicker section. When clipping, *stay away from the thick part of the claw,* or your cat will let out a howl when you try to cut. Cutting into that part of the claw really hurts! On the other hand, clipping off the narrow, pointed part of the claw, below the thick section, doesn't hurt a bit. When you look closely at the thick section of the nail, you'll see a vein. Always clip the nail just below where the vein stops so that you don't sever it.

Note: It's not necessary to clip all of the cat's claws the first time you try this technique. Just clip a few at a time until your cat becomes used to the idea. Eventually you'll be able to clip all the nails at one sitting—with ease.

With this approach clipping claws is painless and can be compared to clipping your own fingernails. As long as you follow the above procedure—and soothe rather than restrain your cat as you work—you should become an expert clipper in no time. Clipping nails is a weekly routine for Crudge, Scruff, and me!

An important device that can help keep your cat's claws duller *and* provide him with some good exercise is the *scratching post.* You can buy one at a cat show or in a pet store, or you can make your own. Usually catnip is rubbed into a smooth board, and then the board is placed flat on the floor or attached to a wall. The board should be anchored in some way so that it won't move around as the cat works on it. A very effective, inexpensive kind of scratching post can be made of a piece of corrugated cardboard. Also, as I indicated in the previous chapter, another inexpensive homemade scratching post can be made with an old piece of carpet. Just attach it to a two-by-four-foot board and let your cat scratch away!

FUR

A cat's coat should be groomed at least once a week, both to improve his appearance and to prevent the possibility that he'll swallow a fur ball. Cats will groom themselves by licking their coats, and if there is a great deal of excess hair, they may swallow it and cause problems in their intestines. Surgery may even be required to remove the obstruction. If your cat has swallowed a fur ball, it's best to give him a commercial medicine that you can buy for this purpose in a pet store, or just try putting some Vaseline on the tip of his nose. These substances will help lubricate the esophagus and enable him to pass the fur ball more easily.

Caution: *Don't* feed your cat mineral oil to help him get rid of the fur ball. Mineral oil can get into his lungs and cause damage there.

How do you groom your cat? First, remember the most fundamental of all cat-care rules—*patience!* (If you have a shorthaired pet, the task is easy.) Next, present yourself to the cat in a calm, gentle way. Stroke her and talk soothingly. Continue to talk as you use a small rubber brush to go over the entire coat. You can employ specially designed brushes or combs with fine teeth that are set close together. This type of instrument helps remove fleas.

As an alternative, you can use a grooming glove, which

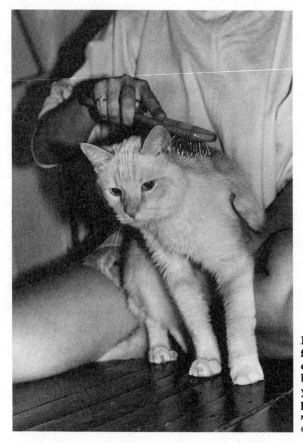

Brushing your cat's fur can lead to a closer relationship between you and your cat and help to prevent fur balls.
MIKE POTTER   Copyright © 1992

may be purchased at a cat show or in a pet store. Or you can use an ordinary cloth glove, which should be dampened. Use your gloved hand to run the cat's coat against the grain of the fur, and then with the grain. This helps to get loose hair out. You can begin this process when your cat is resting peacefully in your lap.

The Longhaired Challenge   Longhaired cats, such as Persians, present more of a grooming challenge. It's best to begin grooming a longhair at the most pleasant places, such as the neck and cheeks. Then, move from head to toe, concentrating at the end on the tougher areas, where the hair is matted. You can break up severely matted clumps with scissors, which should have blunt ends, or by using a wide-tooth comb.

When breaking up a mat in your cat's coat, gently begin at the outer edges of the mat and work your way toward the cat's skin. Repeat the process until the mat is gone. This process is the same as the approach you would use to work a knot out of your own hair.

When you reach the back part of the cat, try to groom the outer thighs first because the hair tends to be smoother there. Then move to the inner thighs, where the hair may become more twisted. To get to the inner leg, you should gently hold up the tail and the leg.

The best comb for a Persian is a deep, wide-toothed, metal instrument. This enables you to get down to the skin and massage it with the teeth. Also, any brush you use on a longhair should be slick, so that it moves as easily as possible along and through the coat.

It's also helpful to sprinkle on some baby powder or a similar commercially produced substance made especially for cats. The powder will help you comb out debris and will enable the comb to move more smoothly through the fur.

Grooming the underside of a cat can be tricky. You'll have to elevate him, such as by getting him to stand up on a table. Also, as you work, it will be necessary to raise the tail to give you access to the hair around his rear, which can become matted.

Finally, don't forget the tail itself. Move your brush smoothly and gently through the hair, from the base of the tail to the end.

Note: If your cat's hair is extremely matted, and you can't seem to do a good job on it, you may have to hire a professional groomer. After the groomer is finished, ask him to show you how to comb your cat, and then you try to be more regular about it (remember, at least once a week!).

The Eyes and Ears   To complete the grooming, you should clean any accumulated matter off the tear ducts—but again, be gentle! Use a soft, damp cloth, and put yourself in the cat's paws. You wouldn't like to have someone scrubbing away in a rough fashion at your eyes! Your cat won't appreciate that either.

As for the ears, clean only the outer area by using a cotton swab dipped in a solution constituted of one-half hydrogen peroxide, one-half alcohol. If you notice wax in the ears, you might try wetting a cotton swab with wheatgerm oil and then let the cat smell it. Next, touch her ear gently with the swab and begin to remove the wax gently. If the wax is deep in the ear, or if you notice a foul smell, see your vet. It's possible your cat may have an ear infection.

As you're working on an ear, you may notice some ear mites, which are creepy little critters that reside just under the surface of the ears. These are most commonly found in kittens and should be removed by a veterinarian.

To Bathe or Not to Bathe?   As a general rule, owners should not bathe their cats. The cats do all their necessary bathing by licking themselves. Of course it's quite all right to remove dirt or excrement that the cat may have missed with a wet cloth. But if you think your pet needs a real dousing, see a professional groomer or your vet.

Despite this advice, I have had several friends who have successfully bathed their cats in a tub, and I bathe Crudge. In fact one woman told me she has a hard time keeping her cat out of the tub, especially when she is preparing to take her own bath. Apparently her cat just dives right in!

FLEAS

During the grooming process you may encounter some fleas. It's hard to see fleas because they are so small, but you may notice them in the form of black, pepperlike material around the base of the tail or on the underbelly. Or you may see the powdery, white remains of flea excrement. The most common indication of fleas is a cat that scratches or licks itself regularly in a particular area.

If you decide your cat has fleas, the chances are your house is infested, too, and this means that a systematic, serious counterattack on both your pet's fur and the infected parts of your house is in order. You'll have to bathe your cat with a special, medicated shampoo and also spray the animal. Special antiflea combs or brushes, which are treated with appropriate medication, can also be useful. But be sure that the shampoo or spray you use is designed specifically for cats! Using a flea product that is made for dogs may cause an allergic or poisonous reaction or otherwise harm the health of your cat.

The cat with fleas will have to be treated at least two to three times because you can't kill the eggs, only the fleas that have already hatched. In other words, several waves of shampooing or spraying will be necessary over several weeks to take care of the problem.

In addition to dealing with your cat's fleas, you'll have to clean up the cat's environment, including your home and yard. It may even be necessary to call in a professional exterminator. The best approach is to vacuum the floor over a period of several consecutive days, with a particular emphasis on those areas where the cat spends most of her time. Also, you should spray those areas with an antiflea insecticide. Be sure to throw away the vacuum bag you've used, and also get rid of any throw rug or blanket used by the cat.

The reason for this systematic attack is based on the egg cycle of the flea. While you may kill the fleas on your cat, others may have laid eggs on your carpet and furniture. These eggs will hatch and the offspring will hop right back on your cat. To keep the eggs from becoming full-grown fleas, you need to vacuum your home and empty or throw the vacuum bag out right away. Also, you'll probably have to repeat the complete process of deflea-ing your cat and vacuuming your home once a week for several weeks. Keep at it until your cat and your home are completely flea-free.

Is Your Cat Well Fed?

Recently I was invited to dinner at the home of a friend who is a cat owner. As it happened, he had forgotten to feed the cat, and as we talked and talked, the cat grew hungrier and hungrier.

Finally the cat jumped up on a counter in the kitchen and assumed a hunter's position. When the owner walked in to get some more food for us, the cat lashed out, claws and all. The moral of this story: If you don't want to be attacked by your pet, feed it!

Even if you're an owner who remembers to feed the cat, the question you may still ask yourself is, Am I feeding my cat the *right* foods?

Generally speaking, people food does not make good cat food. Table scraps typically provide one-third fewer calories than regular, commercially prepared cat food. This means that the cat on this diet usually won't take in enough fuel to function properly; and also, she'll most likely fail to receive sufficient nutrients.

Still, it's not so easy to convince a cat that people food isn't good for her. A cat owned by one of my viewers had a deep craving for cheese. She would do *anything* for cheese. When a young, preschool boy in the home was served a grilled cheese sandwich, he literally had to walk around the room while he was eating. Otherwise he would become an easy target for the cat. In fact one day the cat stood up on her hind legs, with the front legs against the boy's chest, and walked him backward against a wall. She then proceeded to take the sandwich away from the youngster and eat it.

Cats can certainly be aggressive about trying to eat your food, but resist them! Instead buy a commercially prepared cat food at your local supermarket, pet store, or veterinarian office, either dry or canned. Grown cats should be fed once or twice a day; kittens should eat more often, about three to four times a day. As for amounts, here are some guidelines:

- 5–8 ounces of canned food
- 2–4 ounces of semimoist food
- 2–3 ounces of dry food

Another rule of thumb is to feed your cat the amount he will eat comfortably in a sitting of about fifteen to thirty minutes.

Many owners like to place a mixture of canned, semimoist, and dry food in the dish—one-half of each of the above amounts—just to give the cat some variety. Place a helping in a low dish with a separate *fresh* water dish nearby. It's usually best to feed the cat in the morning and then again in the evening. The low dish helps the cat keep the food off his chin and thus avoid cat acne. That's right!

A cat can easily develop pimples simply by having a dirty chin.

One veterinarian has suggested to me that it's also wise to leave some dry food out all the time. This way the cat can crunch away on it if he gets hungry between meals or at night. A nice aspect of feeding cats is that they usually eat only what they need.

Should You Ever Feed Your Cat Human Food?   The regular staple of the cat's diet shouldn't be people food. But it's all right to give a cat an occasional morsel of *cooked* meat, such as chicken gizzards or livers.

Also, some cats are nuts on the subject of seafood. Mackerel is especially potent in attracting cats and may be used to stimulate the appetite of a poor eater. But be sure you don't fall into the trap of giving a fish lover an all-fish diet. That would be unbalanced and would include a deficiency in vitamin E as well as other nutrients. (Some cats, by the way, *hate* fish. Or they may think they like it, but they really are allergic to it. Fish can cause eczema in some cats.)

In general, cats required more protein and fat than we do because of their high metabolism. So, specially prepared cat food should be the staple of your pet's diet.

What to Do About a Finicky Eater   Some cats, like some humans, just won't eat enough. It seems impossible to find a food that will tantalize them.

To take care of this problem, you should try a form of gentle force-feeding. First, begin stroking your cat to make sure she is completely calm. Then take a small, pea-sized piece of food and place it on one finger. Show the food to the cat as you stroke it.

Next place a finger from your opposite hand into the side of the cat's mouth This will cause the cat to open his mouth. Finally very slowly slip the food that is on your other finger into the cat's mouth and rub it behind the teeth on the palate. You don't want to surprise the cat; just move very deliberately and gently.

Admittedly this is a rather slow way to feed a finicky cat, but at least the animal will get some food into his system. A cat can fast for five days without harm, so you might allow her not to eat for four days before you try this force-feeding technique.

Note: Sometimes, a cat will eat too little or too much because he's sick. There may be a hormonal problem, an overactive thyroid gland, or some other disease. These conditions can be diagnosed only by a veterinarian. To help him make his judgment, you should be prepared to provide him with a complete medical history of your pet when you take the animal in for a checkup. In addition, close observation of your cat's behavior when he is well will alert you to the first signs of illness.

The Fat Cat   The opposite problem to the finicky feline involves the one that eats too much and becomes obese. Sometimes a cat may get fat because he doesn't get enough exercise. In this case it's up to the owner to increase the intensity of the animal's physical activity—a responsibility that we'll discuss in more detail in a later chapter.

Also, it may be necessary to cut back on the amount of food that the cat is eating or to change his diet. But I would recommend that you check with your vet and ask him to design a healthy weight-loss regimen for your pet.

Most cats average eight to ten pounds. Of course some large cats, such as the Maine Coon, will weigh much more. In general, if you find your cat weighs much over ten pounds, you should see your vet to be certain your pet doesn't have a problem with obesity.

A diet prescribed by a veterinarian may focus on weight

loss, preventing heart disease, countering bladder problems, or a variety of other health objectives.

Yes, cats have many of the same health concerns that we do! It's been estimated that two out of five cats in the United States are overweight, and many also have heart disease and bladder ailments. Others suffer from weak jawbones and loss of teeth because of a lack of sufficient minerals in their food. Many of these conditions can be detected through regular medical exams, and they may be corrected through special dietary prescriptions.

The Milk Myth   A final note on feeding your cat: Don't be tricked by the milk myth! In fact milk can cause diarrhea in cats, and in large quantities it may even kill them! So stick with water, and stay away from milk.

How About That Litter Box?

The third main area that signals a caring cat owner and a satisfied cat is the condition of the litter box. Many people secretly evaluate the housekeeping ability—and even the hygiene—of friends and relatives by the condition of the bathroom. The same principle applies to the cat's bathroom, the litter box. The basic principle for the litter box is to keep it clean. If you fail to clean out the box every other day and change the litter about once a week, the cat may stop using the box.

The box should be about six inches deep and should be placed in a secluded, quiet location. Cats need privacy, too. Young cats or kittens may need several pans in the house, perhaps one on every floor. This preference is similar to the human custom of using more than one bathroom. Then, as the kittens become accustomed to using a litter box, the number of boxes can be reduced.

What goes into the box? A clay-type litter is commonly used, and baking soda is scattered on the bottom of the box. Male cats that haven't been neutered will give off a bad odor; but when they are neutered, the odor goes away. Cats are basically very clean creatures. They like to bury their excrement—hence the need for some litter to allow them to dig. But remember, if the litter gets dirty, the cat won't use it. So it's imperative that you keep the litter clean.

When it comes to litter for my cat Crudge, I *love* the clumping-type litter! While at first glance, it seems expensive, it actually pays off in the long run because you don't use very much. It lasts a long time and is easy to clean with a pooper-scooper type of tool.

As you clean out the pan a clump at a time, the litter will be slightly depleted. All you have to do is add a little litter to your cat's box, enough to keep it at least two inches deep, rather than throw all the litter away and begin again.

I have found that a great way to clean Crudge's box is to scoop out his excrement in clumps, and put it in a small, empty bag. (The bags you bring your vegetables home in from the grocery store work very well.) Then tie up the bag and throw it away. Even after you remove the clumps, there will be enough litter for your cat to be happily house-trained.

Even though the package labels on the clumping litter suggest that you can flush the "clumps" down the toilet, I don't. In my mind that would be similar to flushing handfuls of sand down the toilet. Eventually, I'm sure that much sand would cause havoc on your plumbing.

Another simple litter-cleaning tip: Take a large garbage bag and slide the litter pan into it, end of pan into end of bag, almost as though you are throwing the litter pan away. Place the litter pan on the floor and adjust the bag so it is indented into the litter box. Pour the litter into the pan, on top of the bag and voilà! You have an easy-to-clean litter pan! The first day Crudge moved in, I prepared his litter pan just like this and to my joy I had an instantly trained house pet and a pan easy to clean!

The big garbage bag will help you in two ways. When your cat digs in his litter, the excess will be caught in the bag. Also, when the litter is ready to be changed, you can just pick up the garbage bag containing the litter and throw it away.

In some cases a cat may also stop using the litter box because he's sick. A painful urinary problem, for example, may cause him to urinate elsewhere because the box reminds him of his discomfort. A failure to use the litter box is one of the main reasons that owners have their cats put to sleep, when usually a cat is trying to tell its owner it doesn't feel well. Medical treatment or a simple surgical procedure may bring the cat back to full health. Some cats, for instance, may have stones blocking their urinary tract. When the stones are removed, they go back to using the box.

Finally, you may find that your cat stops using the box and is spraying different parts of the house when something about the household has changed. A new pet may have been introduced into his environment; or perhaps there is a new baby or a new spouse. Cats, as you now know, are territorial creatures, and the animal may just be feeling insecure and experiencing a need to "stake out" his territory. When he gets used to the change, he'll stop spraying and go back to the box.

You can probably think of other ways that owners show they care for their cats. These are just special quirks that anyone might notice. A more subtle, but still very important question that can indicate the degree of care an owner has for his cat is this: How well has he *trained* his pet?

CHAPTER FIVE

FELINE U AND YOU!

Is it possible to train a cat?

Pet owners who see dogs heel, fetch, roll over, and beg—and then observe cats being totally unresponsive to any commands—may wonder. In fact the common wisdom is that even though cats are pretty smart, they can't be trained.

This is wrong! It's true that cats often don't respond as readily as dogs to human instruction efforts. But still, it's possible to establish your own, reasonably effective "Feline U" at home and move your cat toward a degree in Higher Pet Education.

Beware of the Uneducated Cat!

A cat without any training *may* turn out to be a fairly well-behaved, loving pet, but you can't count on this result! Consider the case of Clarence, a large, gray tabby who was the pet of some friends of mine.

Clarence's peculiar, antisocial habits emerged when he was just a kitten, and as the years passed, he grew more and more undisciplined. He liked to "lie in wait" on top of doors that were ajar in various rooms. And I do mean "in wait." Some wild, untamed, hunting gene must have jarred loose in Clarence, because his main activity on top of those doors was to watch for unsuspecting humans who passed through and take a swipe at their heads. As far as I know, no one was ever badly hurt, but guests usually remained warily on their toes, especially when they were near a passageway.

Clarence's favorite hunting ground was the top of the bathroom door, an excellent place to attack newcomers who were certainly not expecting to encounter an attack cat. On more than one occasion these guests came running out of the bathroom screaming about "a wild animal in the john."

Clarence was also quite fond of human food—but he didn't wait to be served at mealtime. His human overseers began to realize they had a serious problem on their hands when this cat was just a kitten. They left a chocolate cake unattended in Clarence's presence for a few minutes just before a big holiday dinner. The frosting on the cake was cooling, and the cook stepped out of the dining room to see to some other culinary matters. When she returned, however, she found only about a third of the cake still intact, with crumbs spread all over the table and floor. Clarence was sitting over on the sofa, looking very happy and licking a huge belly.

Clarence also had a thing for vegetables. Whenever he got a chance, he would raid the cupboards for bags of peas (his favorite). On one occasion he brazenly walked into the kitchen while dinner was being prepared and set his sights on some corn that was cooking on the stove. He hopped up on the counter, stuck a paw down into the boiling water, and flipped an ear onto the floor. Then, he sat down in the middle of the kitchen, with a cook and a couple of guests watching wide-eyed, and proceeded to clean the cob of every morsel of corn. He actually ate each row of kernels like a typewriter carriage, wiping out one yellow line and then moving on to the next.

Things gradually grew even worse. Clarence didn't limit his foraging to the kitchen. He once stole an entire stalk of broccoli off a guest's dinner plate. Other times he would pester the family for peas, which he loved so much, until they gave him some from their plates. If they delayed, he would hop up and swipe them right off the table.

Finally, these pet owners knew that Clarence's activities had passed the line from mischief to high crimes and misdemeanors when he took an entire turkey carcass off the carving board. Some Thanksgiving! Not only was the dinner ruined; so was the floor, which now had a trail of grease and dressing where Clarence had dragged the bird.

Unfortunately by this time Clarence's behavior had deteriorated too far to do anything about it. My friends loved their cat, and they just decided to put up with him— and warn their friends and relatives to watch out for his misbehavior. He died a few years later, at the happy, rebellious age of sixteen, a thoroughly undisciplined, unregenerate feline.

What can be done to prevent your pet from becoming another Clarence? It all begins with drawing some lines between acceptable and unacceptable conduct.

The Beginning of Discipline: Draw Some Lines!

Cats are a lot like little kids because they don't really talk our language, and they understand only broad, clear directions about their conduct. It doesn't do a bit of good to sit a one- or two-year-old child down in front of you and try to explain how his bad behavior violates the codes of good Judeo-Christian conduct. Nor will she understand why her current mischief, if uncorrected, may later become serious social offenses.

The same observation applies to a cat or any other pet. You *can* train your cat to be a good citizen, but *only* if you're clear and consistent. Also, it's not necessary to become an expert animal trainer or cat psychologist to get the point across. Let me illustrate with a rather wild Siamese named Arnold.

Arnold was owned by Jane, a young single woman who treated him as an equal human being. The two were inseparable, and the cat could do anything he wanted around the house. There really were no limits.

But then Jane married Bill, and Arnold's true colors emerged. While Jane and Bill were dating, Arnold had seemed to be on his good behavior. He spent many hours curled up in the boyfriend's lap or playing with him on the floor. But things changed dramatically when Jane and Bill began to share the apartment. From Arnold's viewpoint, that was taking the relationship a step too far. Bill was always underfoot, occupying Jane's time and attention and invading Arnold's previously exclusive territory in various parts of the apartment.

Arnold became increasingly irascible and unfriendly toward Bill. Finally, he went over the edge one night when Bill and Jane were lying in bed together. The couple heard speeding *thump-thump-thumps,* and before they knew what was happening, Arnold had pounced on the bed and chomped on Bill's toes. Then the cat was gone like a flash. The attacks continued for two or three nights, and finally, despite Jane's attempts to make light of the matter, Bill decided he had to take decisive action. What Arnold was doing was not only wrong, it was dangerous. So Bill resolved to let him know in no uncertain terms.

When the next attack began, with a hurried *thump-thump-thump,* Bill was ready. He waited in the dark until the cat pounced on his toes. Arnold did get in a painful nip, but he also caught a swat from Bill's hand. The animal wasn't hurt at all. But he was shocked, probably more by Bill's counterattack and sudden movement than anything else.

That was the last time that Arnold attacked Bill. The cat even seemed more friendly than before. But whenever Bill made a sudden movement with his arm or hand, Arnold shied away. He remembered clearly the consequences of misconduct.

Now, please understand this: I'm *not* advocating pet abuse! Hitting a cat or any other animal with undue force or without just cause is a deplorable act. But sometimes it's necessary to make a physical statement that says, "You've gone too far, and now I want you to stop it!" You'll be doing your cat—and your family and guests— a major favor if you let your cat know clearly what's acceptable and safe conduct and what isn't.

But how do you know how far to go with this kind of discipline? And how do you design an overall educational program for your cat? As you'll see, a physical response of the type Bill used may sometimes be necessary, but should always be reserved only for use as a last resort.

The Major Components of a Cat's Education

There are three basic approaches that will enable you to control or train your cat: (1) structuring his environment; (2) using positive reinforcement to condition him to do the right thing; and (3) physical discipline.

APPROACH #1: STRUCTURING
THE ENVIRONMENT

You can do a great deal to shape your pet's environment so that he automatically does the right thing. For example, if you put up a scratching post with catnip rubbed into it, you'll lure your pet away from your best drapes or furniture—and you'll keep his claws dulled so that damage to your home or guests is less likely. Regular clipping of claws is another step that owners should take to minimize the cat's tendency to scratch where he shouldn't.

Somtimes it's necessary for an owner to spend some time analyzing his pet's habits and habitats and then to reorganize some part of the house so that the misbehavior becomes impossible. A cat named Dorian provides us with a good example of this principle.

Dorian got into the habit of doing what any intelligent, playful cat might do: taking glittery jewelry and hiding it. He was especially active around Christmas time, with half-wrapped presents in various rooms, or attractive packages under the tree, or decorations *on* the tree.

The best defense against Dorian was to put items that would be particularly attractive in a heavy drawer or lockbox that he couldn't open. Also, the Christmas tree had to be decorated beginning at a point well out of Dorian's reach. Fortunately he didn't choose to climb up the branches to reach the bulbs and other decorations.

But even the greatest care won't completely stymie a clever cat. Dorian's owner, Liz, bought her mother-in-law a silver-chain necklace. But she had trouble wrapping it because a couple of times Dorian actually opened the box when the owner's back was turned and took the jewelry away to a favorite hiding place.

Liz had done her homework, however. She had watched Dorian's movements on several occasions and knew that the cat's favorite cache was a box he kept in a dark corner of the den. So every time the pet would take the necklace, the owner could head for the box and retrieve it.

Finally, the necklace was securely boxed, wrapped, and placed under the tree, and there it remained for the several days remaining before Christmas. When Christmas morning finally arrived, Liz handed the box to her mother-in-law, who promptly opened the present, shook out the wrapping, and turned the box upside down.

"There's nothing in this box," she said.

When Liz examined the package, she noticed some tiny tooth marks on the paper. So she headed immediately to Dorian's hiding place in the den, opened the cat's box, and pulled out the necklace. No one ever figured out how Dorian had opened the present because it had seemed quite securely wrapped. But with a smart, willful cat, almost anything is possible.

I suppose the moral of this story is that no matter how much you try to control a cat's environment, there will always be some way the animal can find to thwart your efforts. That's why additional approaches to training a cat are necessary.

Of course, in this situation, any other type of training would probably have been useless. With cats, there's no concept of "Thou shalt not steal"—at least I don't think there is. It's possible that some creative conditioning technique might have caused Dorian to stop his pilfering, but I doubt it. Those shiny, pretty baubles would probably have just been too tempting for even the most educated feline to resist.

A final point on structuring your cat's environment: Always be cautious when cats are in the same place with small children, especially when those children are visitors or new to the household. As a general rule, *never* leave a cat, a dog, or any other active and potentially dangerous pet alone with a small child. No matter how much training the animal may have been given, there is always the possibility that the child will do something to annoy. The result may be a painful or even tragic bite or swipe of those sharp claws.

So in the last analysis, some situations make it necessary to lock up or secure the things you don't want your cat to have, or to separate the people you want to protect. In short, you may have to shut off certain opportunities or temptations completely, or the cat's natural curiosity, playfulness, or aggressiveness will take over and create all sorts of problems.

APPROACH #2: POSITIVE REINFORCEMENT

One of the best ways to train a cat (or any other animal, for that matter) is through positive reinforcement. In other words, when a cat performs a desirable act, you should reward him with praise, in addition to providing some stroking, a morsel of food, or a little catnip.

For example, contrary to popular opinion, cats can be trained in much the same way as dogs to heel, sit, stay, keep off the furniture, or come. The reasons that you don't see more cats performing these feats is simply that their owners haven't taken the time to educate them.

How do you do it? By being very patient. Here are some more suggestions:

• Select *one* behavior that you want to teach, and stick with it, twice a day for about fifteen minutes a day, until the animal can respond reasonably well to your command.

• Gently move the cat to the desired position, and

then repeat cleary the command that relates to that position.

For example, with one hand under your cat's chin and the other on his hindquarters, gently lift his head. At the same time, push his rear to the ground and say, "Sit." When your cat is in the sitting position, praise him by saying, "Good cat," or something to that effect. Eventually your cat will understand your command and will sit when you tell him to sit. (It also helps to "cup" your cat's bottom with your hand as you tell him to sit.)

Continue to repeat this process until he is actually sitting on command. When he reaches the position, immediately reward him. It may be enough just to say, "Good cat!" several times and pet him, or you could provide him with a favorite food. But be cautious when you are rewarding your cat with food. Too much can lead to obesity, which can lead to serious health problems such as heart disease.

There are also many complex movements that can be taught to a cat after he has learned the basic commands, such as sit, come, and stay. With complex movements, such as fetching, you may have to break up the behavior into its component parts and then teach and reward each part.

For example, you might hold the cat, throw a wadded-up paper ball several feet away from you, say "Fetch," walk the cat over to the ball, and put it into his mouth. The cat should then be rewarded at this point for successfully completing the first stage of the movement.

Next, you might say, "Bring!" and walk the cat back to your beginning position.

After the cat gets used to this back-and-forth movement with you, you can try tossing the ball and saying "Fetch-Bring" together. If he hesitates at the ball repeat

"Bring!" and reward him when he comes back to you with it. Or if he runs over, picks the ball up, and returns it to you in one continuous movement, he also gets his reward.

Finally, you'll probably find that the cat will be able to execute the entire movement after you just say "Fetch!"

• *Only reward* a cat during this type of training. *Never* rely on punishment. A negative response from you sends a mixed message to your feline friend.

• One of the best rewards is to pet the cat and talk soothingly to him *after he obeys*. During the training session don't reward him this way if he's not responding. The main idea is to reinforce the desired behavior, and he won't be able to distinguish between what you want and what you don't want if you reward him for everything.

Another effective reward is a morsel of favorite food, such as a small piece of fish. Slice several portions before the training session begins and then feed them to your pet when he does what you require.

You'll probably find that it takes more patience to educate a cat than it does to work with a dog. But don't despair! The results will be worth all the time and effort, and once your cat learns how to respond or behave, he won't forget.

• Limit each training session to a few minutes, or as long as the cat can take it without becoming irritable or totally distracted. Also, restrict the training to no more than about two of these sessions per day, one in the morning and one in the afternoon.

• Devote some time *every* day to the training. If you allow several days to elapse between sessions, the cat will forget what he's learned, and effective, speedy conditioning will become difficult, if not impossible.

• When your cat has learned one behavior, go immediately to another. In other words, when he's learned to sit, you might try getting him to heel. This way he'll get used to the idea of "attending class," with you as the instructor.

• Choose the behavior you want to teach in order of increasing complexity. Don't start off with fetching, which is a rather complex behavior. Instead, try teaching your cat different basic skills, in an order such as this: sit; come; heel; stay; keep away from certain parts of the house, such as the furniture; fetch; and finally, perform various tricks, such as jumping through a hoop.

Note: As with humans, a task that may be easy for one cat may be difficult for another. You'll have to be sensitive to your cat's personality and abilities, and flexible in the order in which you educate him.

• Don't expect perfection; just look for progress. For example, if a cat goes from obeying your "sit" command one out of five times to two out of five times, you're succeeding!

As strange as it may seem, it is possible to teach your cat to do all kinds of tricks. I have two close friends Joy and Tom who actually play fetch, catch, bat the ball, and baseball with their cat Shawn on a regular basis. Shawn enjoys all of these games and will play them until she has had enough exercise.

To begin with, Shawn will come when her name is

called. Whenever she hears her name, she just waltzes into the room as though to say, "Yes?"

Also Shawn loves to play catch. She literally goes to the top of the stairs and her owners throw a small wadded-up paper ball to her. Shawn catches the ball, in *mid-air*, in *both* of her paws. She then places the ball beside her and bats the ball back down the steps to her owners! Really! And this game can go on for quite some time.

Another game Shawn loves to play is "fetch." Shawn's owners toss a ball down the hallway and she runs to get the ball, brings it back to her human parents, and drops it by their feet. Shawn does this over and over until she gets tired.

Yet another game frequently played in this household—as if the others aren't enough—Joy and Tom discovered quite by accident: Shawn loves to play "baseball," and it's now a family activity. One day Tom and Joy were tossing one of Shawn's toys back and forth in a friendly game of catch. Lo and behold, Shawn began jumping in the air to intercept the toy and bat it back to the person who tossed it. Shawn was determined. She jumped very high into the air to try to bat the toy each time it was tossed. Today she really enjoys this game as much as her human parents, who laugh watching their "baseball" cat.

This cat loves to play! And all of this playing gives her great exercise and a closer relationship with her owners.

Even though Joy and Tom didn't intentionally set out to teach Shawn these activities, they were able to train this top-notch feline simply by watching her behavior and building on her natural activities. This is another method of teaching your cat to do tricks. You and your cat can play the same types of games at your own Feline U.

APPROACH #3: PHYSICAL DISCIPLINE

Sometimes, when all else fails in the attempt to curb bad behavior, it's necessary for an owner to communicate more sternly or even physically with a cat.

In the earlier example in this chapter, Bill felt that there was absolutely no other way he could have taught the cat Arnold that his toe biting was out of order. The cat was acting in a potentially dangerous way, and he had to be stopped in his tracks. In fact Bill's swat to Arnold was a major turning point that set their relationship back on a more productive path.

But usually there's no reason for a cat-human relationship to reach this point if the owner pays more attention to training at an earlier stage. Begin by speaking sharply and in a deep voice to the cat when he's doing something that is unacceptable. For example, if your cat likes to play with food in your kitchen, as Clarence in a previous illustration did, you might say "No!" or "Stop!' or "Out!" sharply. Let him have a full blast of your voice. Don't be friendly at this point or he may misinterpret. At the same time, remove him physically from the forbidden location.

Instead of giving in to physical punishment when your cat misbehaves, make a loud noise near his head. You might clash two pan lids together or smack your hand against a newspaper and at the same time say loudly, "No!" These sounds should quickly get your cat's attention and stop the undesirable behavior.

As I type this section of *Living with Cats,* Crudge has come to visit. He has meowed loudly, and instead of jumping into my lap, he has learned to wait until I either pick him up or tell him "Up." He is now sitting in my lap, purring, as he watches the cursor zoom by on the computer screen. The first time Crudge sat on my lap as I worked, he tried to attack the screen and stop my hands from typing. He learned very quickly that this was unacceptable behavior. All it took was a few loud "No's!" from me and simultaneously placing him on the floor. Now, he seems to have learned to sit fairly still or fall asleep as I work.

If a cat simply won't stay out of mischief through other means, and his behavior is threatening the order or safety of the rest of the household, you'll have to be firmer. One of the most effective means that a number of owners use when nothing else works is a squirt gun. If you've told your cat not to climb on the drapes, and all your positive reinforcement, sharp commands, or other efforts don't work, just let her have it with one, well placed squirt and bark out "No!" simultaneously. That should do the trick. Every owner I've known who has used this technique has said you only have to squirt once or twice and the lesson is learned.

Finally I recommend that you *not* give the cat a physical whack *unless* he's being dangerous to you or someone else. But if he swipes, scratches, or bites someone without being provoked, for example, he must be taught that this behavior is totally unacceptable. Remember, a cat wound is more likely to become infected than a wound from any other pet, and you simply can't allow that kind of behavior to exist. There must be no delay between his transgression and your response. Otherwise he may not get the point. A quick *light* rap with your hand will be enough to teach him he's out of line—without risking injury.

Special Ed.

In addition to the above courses of instruction, there is a kind of "special education" curriculum for cats that I think every owner should explore. A couple of important "special ed." areas are litter training; and traveling.

Litter Training   Litter training, which we've already covered in some detail in the previous chapter, is quite easy because cats like to have a special, private place to go to the bathroom. Still, you have to set the litter box up properly, as already described. Otherwise, the cat will establish his own procedures, and that may involve bad habits that are hard to break.

When you begin litter training with a kitten, remember that you may have to set out a small litter box in several rooms or on several floors of the house. As the kitten grows older, you can reduce the number of boxes until she has just one, placed in a quiet spot of your choice. Many owners make the mistake of placing the litter box in a high-traffic area in their home—and can't figure out why the cat won't use the box. A cat needs and likes privacy, just like humans!

If you live in a large house or apartment, your cat should have more than one litter box in different areas of your home. For example, you might place one upstairs and one downstairs.

The litter, which may be constituted of clay or some other gravellike material that you can buy in a pet or grocery store, should be scattered loosely in the box. This way the cat can easily cover up his leavings.

Remove excrement from the box daily with a pooper-scooper, and change all the litter in the box every week. Cats are very clean creatures and they can be quite finicky about their hygiene.

Traveling   It's perfectly fine to take a cat with you on a trip, but *always* use a cat carrier, even in the car! These specially designed boxes, which can be purchased in most pet stores and cat shows, give the cat a sense of security. They are the perfect means to keep the cat under control by structuring his environment wisely. Employing a cat

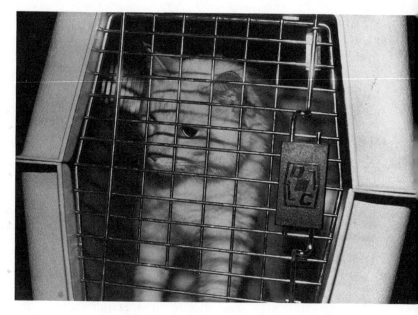

Every cat can learn to love traveling in a carrier.   MIKE POTTER

carrier in your car is extra insurance that your cat won't crawl under the accelerator or brake pedal while you are driving.

The boxes involve a relatively small, enclosed space, sometimes with a cage top. You may be afraid you're mistreating the cat or provoking claustrophobia, but cats aren't like humans in this regard. They like the close environment. Being in a secluded, dark area enables them to stay calm. In fact, if you're traveling by plane, you shouldn't use a carrying box with a cage top because that may be too open for the cat.

If you try to carry a cat in your arms, or put him loose in the backseat of your car, you'll almost certainly be in for trouble. Many cats have interfered with the driver or jumped out of the car window.

When you're going on a short trip in your car, say for

Robert Goulet introduces his Abyssinian, Vincent, to Gale.

less than about three or four hours, you won't need a litter box. But if you plan a long trip, a litter box is a necessity.

As you gain some experience traveling with your cat, you may find, as singer Robert Goulet and his wife, Vera, have, that it's possible to have a red carpet rolled out for your feline. They were recently traveling with their Abyssinian named Vincent when Bob was with the thirtieth anniversary tour of *The Fantastiks*. He told me that he takes Vincent in a small carrying case under his plane seat.

"You're allowed one cat in first class, and one in coach," he said. That means he has to leave his other five cats at home when he's on the road.

He advised not putting the cat in a nonpressured baggage compartment, at least not if you value your pet's health. To Bob's amazement, a cat plane reservation typically costs him fifty dollars, he says, and he also makes a special reservation for the pet in hotels where they stay.

"They'll provide you with a box with kitty litter and dishes with different cat goodies," he said.

Vera and Bob even leave the cat alone in their hotel room, where he has the run of the suite. "I returned one night after leaving Vincent alone and found I had a three-hundred-dollar bar tab—signed with paw prints," he kidded.

That's some cat, Bob.

These are some of the main areas that will help you further your cat's education. But there's also another vast, important area of schooling that might be placed under the heading "Phys. Ed."—an essential course of instruction for the "aerobic cat."

CHAPTER SIX

THE AEROBIC CAT

CATS WERE *CREATED* for exercise. Their forebears in the forests and jungles had to climb, forage, and hunt to survive, and that meant stretching and employing every muscle and ligament.

Like many humans, however, far too many domestic cats have become sedentary. They often don't have mice and other vermin to chase. They may lack access to an outdoor environment, where they can work on their climbing, jumping, and running skills. The end result is that they become soft and flabby. The cat that doesn't do enough exercise inevitably becomes a fat cat—and an unhealthy one that may develop heart problems and other ills.

How can you ensure that your cat will get enough exercise? Turn him into an *aerobic cat,* that's how!

Recent studies have shown that humans live

longer, healthier lives if they engage in aerobic (endurance) activity, such as walking and running, and the same is true of cats. Other studies have established that humans who work at maintaining their muscle mass through strength conditioning have more functional bodies, including stronger bones, as they age. Again, the same goes for cats.

In this chapter I'll provide you with a number of exercise ideas for your cat—as well as for yourself. Some owners may prefer to remain couch potatoes as their cats cavort around them. For these individuals I've provided a "Sedentary Owner's Guide to Cat Workouts." But it's best for the owner as well as the cat to engage in vigorous physical activity, not only because humans need exercise as much as animals but also because it's more *fun* to work out together. Consequently many of the following programs have been suggested with this joint exercise principle in mind.

The Sedentary Owner's Guide to Cat Workouts

If you're just not feeling like running around with your cat—or if physical disability makes it impossible—you should still encourage your pet to do his daily exercise routine. Here are some guidelines that have worked for a number of owners.

The Fishing-Pole Follies   When I was taping one television program, I came across a marvelous little cat toy designed in the shape of a fishing pole. A string was tied to one end, and a small piece of denim was attached to the end of the string. There were two sizes of poles— one about two feet long and one about four feet long. The four foot version could be folded up and put in a suitcase for easy transport when owner and cat are on the move.

I bought one and gave it to a friend who owns an Abyssinian. She would sit in an easy chair and watch TV while holding the fishing pole. Every second or so she would flip the denim "bait" on the end of the pole to one side of the room. Then, she would flip it to the other side. The cat would go crazy with excitement as he chased the denim from one side of the room to the other. He'd jump into the air, pounce on it, and then back off to give the owner a chance to flick it elsewhere.

Clearly cats love this kind of exercise toy—and it's great for their physical conditioning. They get plenty of work on their legs and also improve their endurance capacity if you keep them moving back and forth for several minutes, with no time for rest.

You may be able to find one of these poles and similar toys at your local pet store or at a cat show. Or you could make one yourself quite easily with just three components: a two- to four-foot thin pole, two feet of string or twine, and a colorful piece of ribbon.

The Scratching Post   I mentioned this device in a previous chapter, but the concept bears repeating for a couple of reasons. A scratching post provides terrific exercise for your cat—and protects your furnishings.

A scratching post should be constructed of a smooth wooden board or piece of corrugated cardboard, a couple of feet long and four to six inches wide. The board should be attached firmly to a wall or to the floor so that the cat won't move it about.

One purpose of the post is to provide the cat with a way to wear down his nails. Regular access to a post often makes it unnecessary to clip the cat's claws. Another purpose is daily exercise. Cats build up the muscles in their legs and paws by clawing the board, and the result is a stronger, healthier pet.

The Ball Game   Cats love to bat and chase balls or ball-like objects. But it's important to provide your pet with a *safe* toy, and that means one that is *not* made of rubber, soft plastic, or loose yarn. The cat may swallow pieces of rubber or other substances and choke on them. The best components for a play ball are hard plastic, wood, or even wadded-up paper.

When you've found the right kind of object, you will probably want to buy or make several of them and then toss them about the room to keep your cat constantly on the move.

Walking Your Cat

At the beginning of this book I mentioned Perry Como's practice of taking his cat on regular walks. That's a great idea because walking is one of the best exercises for both pets and humans.

The average person can take off 90 to 100 calories just by taking a brisk, one-mile walk. Furthermore, research done at the Institute for Aerobics Research in Dallas has shown that people who are completely sedentary are more than twice as likely to die of all causes than are those who maintain a minimum level of aerobic fitness. Minimal fitness can be achieved just by taking a fast walk for thirty to forty-five minutes, three to five times per week.

The same principles of health apply to animals, including pet cats. Remember, cats were *not* intended to sit around on people's laps. They are made for activity, and it's up to their owners to ensure that they get plenty of it.

Here's a suggested walking program for you and your cat:

- If you've been relatively inactive or have not engaged in vigorous exercise, get a thorough checkup from your doctor and secure his clearance before you try exercising.

- Get a cat harness that will fit over your cat's head and front legs with a relatively long leash attached. The cat should have some freedom, but shouldn't be able to dart out into the street or otherwise get into danger or mischief.
- Begin your regimen by walking with your cat at least twenty minutes (or until he refuses to move), three to four days a week. You'll need to carry a watch with a second hand.
- Move along at a pace that feels comfortable for your cat. Time yourself from beginning to end of each exercise session.
- Stick with your beginning pace for about two weeks. Then, over the following month, gradually increase the time you spend walking to thirty to forty-five minutes, at least three to four days per week.
- Now begin to walk faster and gradually increase the distance you cover during the time period. There are no limits as to how far or how fast you should walk, other than the internal limits set by you and your cat.

How can you expect your cat to react to this activity? At first he may resist, but don't feel you have to pull and tug him along. Instead you might try walking in circles around him. Or walk forward a few steps, until you come to the end of his leash, and then walk backward a few steps. This way you can continue to benefit from the exercise, even if your cat is being uncooperative.

Before you begin walking your cat outside, your cat will have to first get used to *wearing* the harness. Accomplish this by placing the harness on your cat and letting him walk around the house. Next attach the leash to the harness and walk around the house with your cat. Once your cat becomes accustomed to walking with you around the house, then you can begin your walks outside.

If your cat throws himself on the ground and refuses to move, don't be disappointed—just be patient! This takes time.

If you've secured a sufficiently long leash, you can keep moving easily, even if he decides to pull a long-term sit-down strike on you. The chances are, however, as he sees you moving about him, he'll start moving with you. Remember, your cat may be in worse shape than you are. It may take some conditioning to get him accustomed to moving along with you at a brisk pace.

Cats on the Run

Is it really possible to *run* with your cat? It is indeed. Cats are as able to run as dogs—in fact the cheetah is often cited as the fastest animal in the world. The problem is that many domestic cats spend their entire lives indoors, and as a result they don't get a chance to demonstrate their speed or endurance.

If you're a jogger, or an exerciser who combines walking with jogging, your cat should be able to keep up with you. But if the pet has been mostly sedentary, you'll have to introduce her gradually to vigorous exercise.

As with walking, the equipment you'll need will include a harness, a relatively long leash, and a watch with a second hand. Here's a suggested beginning program, after you've secured clearance for exercise from your physician:

- Set aside three to four days each week, and begin with a twenty-minute workout each day.
- Start by walking briskly for a few minutes. Then jog for as long as you can comfortably manage. Next return to a brisk walk until you catch your breath. After you've recovered, try jogging again for a short distance.
- Continue this alternate walk-jog program for a few weeks, and gradually increase the amount of time you jog. At the same time, decrease the time you devote to walking. Also, extend the total time of your walk-jog workout to thirty to forty-five minutes.
- Within a couple of months you should be able to jog for the entire workout. Then you can increase your jogging speed gradually.

You can expect an out-of-shape cat to refuse to run *or* walk at some point early on in this routine. It's almost inevitable that she will become tired, bored, or want to get out of the harness. If that happens, run in place, or jog in a tight circle around her until she decides to start moving again. Pulling on the leash or trying to force her to get started won't work.

When the cat begins to get into better shape, however, she'll actually look forward to these outings, and you'll probably find she often wants to run along at a faster pace than you can manage. At other times, though, even an aerobically fit cat will become distracted by a bird, person, or other item of interest. In these situations the owner should just revert to running or walking in place or in circles until the pet is ready to move on. If you live in a city, be aware of fast-moving vehicles. Recently, on an evening outing I happened to be holding Crudge when a truck accelerated to get through a traffic light. Crudge was terrified and tried to jump out of my arms. It took me a while to calm him down and resume our walk.

As you can see, working out with a cat requires some accommodation to the interests and needs of the animal, but this fact shouldn't come as any great surprise. If you were running with another human, you'd both have to agree on the route you'd take and the pace at which you'd move. It's similar with a pet. In the long run, by adjusting your workout to your cat's exercise rhythms, you'll find the entire process of aerobic conditioning can be much more interesting than just pursuing an exercise regimen on your own.

The Dancing Cat

In some ways the easiest kind of exercise to do with your cat is some variation on aerobic dancing. If you usually follow a routine demonstrated on a television program or a videotape, you might stimulate your cat by using some of the toys and other devices mentioned in the guidelines for sedentary cat owners.

For example, as you do your aerobic dance program, you could hold one of the cat fishing poles and flick it about while you do your exercises. This way your pet will be encouraged to move around as much as you do.

Another possibility is to wad up a dozen or more pieces of colored paper, put them in a baglike holder around your waist or over your shoulder, and toss them to your cat at regular intervals during the routine. Also, as you move around, you could kick the paper balls about to keep your pet in motion.

The first time I exercised around Crudge I had my hair

in its usual ponytail. In a standing position, I was stretching down to my toes. Suddenly, I had a strange sensation on the top of my head, which was now upside down and between my ankles. The sensation felt as though my ponytail had a fishing weight on it. Slowly looking up, I realized that Crudge was "batting" my ponytail as I stretched downward. I guess he figured "Look! New toy!" The same type of thing happened when I was on my side doing leg lifts. Crudge tried to catch my foot as it went up and down, up and down. (Clever cat!)

I finally decided that when I exercised, I needed to make Crudge a little exercise toy so I could work out and work Crudge out at the same time. The toy was simple and consisted of a chew toy tied to the end of a thick ribbon. Now when I do leg lifts, I dangle the toy in front of Crudge. He plays with the toy and is distracted from my leg lifts. Of course, I lose count on my exercises. However, somehow Crudge and I do get plenty of exercise, and I get many added laughs. Boy! You should see what happens when Scruffette wants to join in the exercise also!

Caution: Be careful to ascertain your cat's whereabouts if you do part of your exercises on the floor. Vigorous exercise can cause a cat to become quite excited, and she may forget how dangerous her claws or teeth can be to you and your safety. She may bolt at you from your blind side and take a playful swipe—which could leave you with a scratch or cut. I have a scar on my arm from one of Crudge's "playful" swipes.

The Obstacle Course

A more complex routine, which can exercise a cat's muscles as well as her endurance capacities, involves, in effect, setting up an obstacle course. A variation that appeals to many human exercisers is called the parcourse. This is a series of stations that requires the participant to do different movements that will increase the strength and stamina of muscles in different parts of the body.

In a human parcourse, for instance, there may be a one-mile running course punctuated by a place to do push-ups, a place for chin-ups, a place for sit-ups, and so on. By the same token, a cat-human parcourse can be set up this way:

- Get your cat a harness with a long leash.
- Lay out a course with events that would interest your cat, such as trees to climb, logs to scale or jump over, and bushes to run through.
- Decide on exercises that you can do while your pet is performing his. For example, you might do some sit-ups while your cat is climbing up to the first limb on a tree. (Note: Be sure that you secure the end of your leash before the cat starts to climb, or you may be climbing the tree or calling the fire department to get him down!)
- Be patient. It will probably take quite a few false starts before you discover the best way for both you and your pet to get adequate exercise on this type of course. If all else fails and you find your cat spending much more time on his obstacles or stations than you do on yours, just jog in place. Remember, you're striving for aerobic and strength conditioning, so you can't lose if you keep your feet moving.

Of course there are many other ways that you can exercise with your cat. If your preference is indoor cycling, for instance, you could make good use of the fishing pole or paper-wad balls to keep your pet moving as you go through your workout.

But I would advise you to avoid involving your cat in outdoor cycling, swimming, or other activities that are inherently more dangerous and unnatural for her. Remember, cats were made mainly to walk, run, jump, and climb, and these activities should be the focus of most of the joint exercise outings you attempt.

CHAPTER SEVEN

IS THERE A DOCTOR IN THE CAT'S HOUSE?

A SICK CAT should always be taken to the vet. But how can you tell if your cat is sick? What are some of the key symptoms of common cat ailments? How can you take steps to *prevent* the prevalent diseases that can threaten your cat's health—and even his life?

To answer these questions, you must become a kind of front-line "cat doc" or health specialist, because *you* are the one who must decide whether or not to call in the veterinarian. The first and most important step is to observe your cat when she is healthy. Be able to recognize her eating, sleeping, and elimination behavior. If you notice a change in any of her patterns, that's a sure sign that something is wrong with the cat's health. At that point it's time to contact the vet.

Getting to Know Your Vet

If you are in the habit of taking your pet in for the required vaccinations and other procedures—and if you tend to contact him when unusual signs or symptoms appear—you're much more likely to provide the cat with better health and a longer life.

I've already mentioned a few points about your relationship with your vet, schedules for shots, and other doctor-related issues. But I want to focus on this aspect of vet-pet interactions because it's so important in helping you *prevent* the onset of many diseases. So here are the highlights:

Vet Visits   The first thing on your agenda after you've acquired a new cat is to take him to the vet for a complete examination.

The vet will schedule a complete set of shots, including those for distemper and rabies. The shots generally begin at age six to eight weeks for kittens. There will also be shots for respiratory viruses and distemper which are usually finished by the time the animal is about sixteen weeks old. Then there will be booster shots once a year after that.

On the first visit the vet will conduct a stool exam for parasites and worms and will also give the cat a leukemia test. These guidelines for an exam apply both to kittens and older cats, though there may be a variation in the schedule of shots for older cats if they have a record of previous vaccinations.

After the first visit a trip to the vet once a year may be enough, unless you notice unusual signs or symptoms, which may indicate an illness. When the pet grows older, you'll probably want to take her in to the vet about twice a year. Older cats have more problems with their teeth and gum disease, and, like older humans, they require more medical attention. Also, the doctor will want to check the older cat's heart.

The Rationale Behind the Visit   I'm a big advocate of taking your pet in for regular visits to the vet. You should go in any time the animal is sick, and at least once a year. This way you can have a medical professional check over your pet and possibly catch illnesses or serious health conditions at an early stage. Also, when your pet does become sick, the vet visit will seem less strange and stressful—to you and maybe even to your cat!

Finally, by keeping in touch with the animal doctor, you'll be more likely to stay alert to common illnesses that are plaguing the local pet community. In addition you'll be apprised of ways that you, as a concerned owner, can respond to prevent health problems from threatening your cat.

Cat Symptoms

Even if you get to know your vet quite well, it's essential to become acquainted with some of the most common health problems that your cat may face. This means knowing the telltale symptoms for certain illnesses so that you can alert the vet when necessary and ask intelligent questions on behalf of your pet. The following are signs, symptoms, and responses to some of the most common diseases and complaints that I've encountered in my dealings with cats, cat owners, and veterinarians.

1 : FOOD AND MEDICINE ALLERGIES

Symptoms: The cat may have vomiting, diarrhea, skin lesions, bumps on the back of the neck, itchiness, or ulcers around the mouth.

Cause: The cat may be allergic to certain human foods, or pet food, or he may be reacting to a new medication or to a new plant in your house.

Response: Contact your vet. If the allergic reaction has just started, you may be able to associate it with some new food your pet has eaten. In such a case, take the food or medicine out of his diet and see what happens.

Caution: If you are removing a medicine, be sure to tell the vet. The vet will want to know what reactions your cat is having to the prescribed medication, so you should compile a list of side effects that seem to be caused by the drug. Most likely the vet will then prescribe a different medication.

In general, cats should not be fed milk, human food, dog food, or anything other than commercial foods that are specially prepared for cats.

2 : FUR BALLS

Symptoms: The cat may vomit or have trouble swallowing.

Cause: While licking or cleaning himself he may have swallowed some of his own fur and created a fur ball. Or he may have swallowed some other foreign object, such as yarn or string. The fur then gets into the stomach or intestines and causes any food the cat eats later to back up.

This problem can be dangerous because the vomiting will cause the cat to lose bodily fluids and electrolytes. If it continues, the cat may even die.

Other possible causes of vomiting include kidney or liver disease, ingestion of poison plants, eating a dead bird or other animal carrying a disease, or eating an insect that has died from a poison in your home.

Response: Don't play doctor at home. Take your pet to the vet immediately. Surgery or other special care may be required.

A note on fumigating your home: Remove all of the

dead bugs immediately. Otherwise your cats are likely to find the bugs, play with and eat them—thus causing a reaction to poison in your cat.

#3: URINARY TRACT PROBLEMS

Symptoms: Your pet may urinate frequently, or urinate only in small amounts, with some straining, or outside of his litter box. There may be blood in the urine; or the cat may not be able to urinate at all.

Cause: These symptoms are often caused by an infection of the urinary tract or sometimes by bladder stones.

Usually, though, it's impossible to identify the precise reason that the problem developed. Some feel that certain cats respond negatively to excessive minerals in their water, or to a virus. Others believe that these difficulties can be traced to a failure of certain cats to drink enough fluids.

Response: Be sure your cat has plenty of clean water to drink and food to eat. If urinary symptoms develop, the vet may prescribe antibiotics to combat an infection, or he may ask you to change the foods or water you're giving your pet.

Young male cats may experience a complete blockage of the urinary tract. In this case the vet must be called in immediately because uremic poisoning may result. With uremic poisoning, the cat may die in just a couple of days.

#4: ABSCESSES

Symptoms: The cat may have a wound that is partially or completely healed on the skin but that nevertheless begins to swell or grow red. The swelling may eventually burst and emit red or yellow fluid.

Cause: Your cat may have been involved in a fight with another animal, and the bacteria from a scratch or bite may remain under the skin. This can cause an infection, which may rupture.

Response: First call the vet and describe the wound, and take your vet's advice. Keep your pet indoors, or supervise her when she's roaming about outside. Male cats should be neutered to lower their aggressive tendencies and thus prevent fights.

If the cat becomes wounded and infected despite your precautions, the vet will prescribe antibiotics to counter the infection and lower any fever.

5 : FLEAS

Symptoms: The cat may scratch or lick constantly at a particular part of the body. Also, though a live flea is hard to detect, you may see black pepperlike material around the base of the tail or on the cat's underbelly.

Cause: Fleas usually become a problem when the cat has been outdoors or in contact with another cat or dog that carries fleas.

Response: Bathe your cat with a medicated shampoo, which you can buy in most pet stores. Also, apply cat flea powder or spray every day. Vacuum every place in your home where your cat has been—and do it several times. The flea eggs may hang around for a while. You may have to repeat the procedure several times, because eggs remain unaffected until hatched. If the problem persists despite your constant efforts, you may want to call in an exterminator.

I'm not a big believer in flea collars because the only time I used one on a cat the results were disastrous. In addition, I have been told many times by those "in the know," that once a flea or tick collar is wet it no longer works.

So what do I do? I give Curmudgeon and Scruffette a

flea bath, one animal after the other, with an aloe-based flea shampoo. If I bathe Scruff first, Crudge hangs around on the floor. When it's his turn I gently lift him into the sink, wet him down, add the shampoo, wash, rinse, get rid of the excess water, dry him off with *two* towels, and then use the hair drier. If Crudge and I are up to it, Crudge then gets his toenails clipped. This whole process takes between fifteen and thirty minutes. Period.

The first time I gave Crudge a bath, my neighbor helped. Since that time I have traveled this road alone. I must admit, Crudge seems to be getting used to this bathing procedure. I begin by holding him by the nape of his neck as I cover him with water. He actually holds farily still throughout, but on occasion he does try to bolt. At that point, I just grab him and say, "No," and he resigns himself to the remainder of the bath.

A few tips for bathing your cat: Use warm water. Once the cat is wet, apply the shampoo first around your cat's neck and rub it in. Fleas run to the neck to hide, so you will trap them by first shampooing your cat around his neck. Next apply shampoo to your cat's body, haunches, legs, underside, and paws, and rub in the shampoo.

Be sure to wash your cat's stomach. The fur is thick there and it becomes a haven for fleas. As you wash your cat, you will see fleas. Go ahead! Take the fleas off your cat. Your cat will feel so very much better.

Usually, you leave a flea shampoo on your cat for five minutes. This is a great opportunity to massage your cat as you shampoo him. Don't be surprised when your cat purrs or contentedly closes his eyes as you shampoo. (Talk about body language!) After the five-minute waiting-and-massage period has lapsed, thoroughly rinse the shampoo off your cat. Because most cat fur is very thick, use your hands to gently squeeze out excess water; then use towels to soak more of the water off your cat. Finally, if you wish, use your hair dryer to complete the process. Brush your cat's fur as you dry him. This will get rid of excess fur. It also makes the drying process faster and helps to prevent fur balls.

The first several times you bathe your cat, expect the following: *You* will be wet! *You* may be clawed! Your *cat* may be frightened. So remember: Have patience. Talk or sing a lullaby to your cat. Singing seems to be a great distraction to Crudge and keeps him calmer (maybe it's just my voice!).

A note about the hair dryer: A cat can dry himself. However, after you have bathed your cat, your cat will be wet literally for hours as he licks himself dry. It is for this reason that I *suggest* using a hair dryer, but it is not necessary. When using the hair dryer, give your cat time to adjust to the sound and the feeling of the air by turning on the hair dryer away from him, and moving it slowly to him, rather than turning it on full blast directly on your cat.

I've got to tell you. Shampooing your cat actually works and I'm finding it an enjoyable experience. After Crudge is dry, he smells great, is very soft, and—the added bonus—has no fleas! Another added plus to shampooing your cat is that it will bring the two of you closer together. I know it sounds weird . . . but it works!

6 : TICKS

Symptoms: Your cat may scratch, or you may see or feel a protruding little lump upon petting or observing your cat's skin.

Cause: Cats usually pick up ticks when they are roaming about outdoors. The ticks may be normal size, so that they look like a small mole stuck onto the skin. Or they may be quite small, deer ticks, which are harder to detect.

Deer ticks may be picked up from deer or mice and can carry the dreaded Lyme disease.

Response: Pull the tick straight out with a pair of tweezers. If the head of the tick remains in the cat's skin, try to get that out, too, to reduce the possibility of infection.

Of course your cat may not like the idea of your digging around in his skin, so the operation may have to wait for the services of the vet. In any case, any cat who has a tick should be taken to the doctor for a complete checkup.

Caution: Diseases, such as Lyme disease, which are transmitted by ticks, can endanger humans; so be careful to keep any cat ticks away from your own skin.

#7: WORMS

Symptoms: The cat may vomit, have diarrhea, lose weight, or otherwise seem sick. Also, inspection of the cat's stool may disclose spaghetti-shaped worms (roundworm) or worms of an exceptionally dark color (possible hook worm). If you notice small, moving, white creatures around the cat's anus, these may be tapeworms.

Cause: Cats may pick up worms by eating mice, fleas, or other infected animals or insects.

Response: Keep your cat's litter box clean at all times and perform a visual inspection of the animal at regular intervals to check for signs and symptoms of worms.

If you suspect the cat has worms, take a sample of the stool to the vet. He will prescribe medication and will provide you with other tips for treatment and prevention at home.

#8: EAR MITES

Symptoms: Bumps may appear just under the surface of the skin in the cat's ears. Kittens are more likely to be affected than adults.

Cause: The mites are often picked up by a kitten as it is nursing from the mother cat.

Response: The vet will have to remove the mites and prescribe medication for home treatment. Also, it's important for the owner to keep the cat's ears quite clean to prevent recurrence.

#9: DENTAL PROBLEMS

Symptoms: An accumulation of hard or discolored matter on the cat's teeth, or redness and soreness of gums, may indicate a dental problem.

Cause: Poor dental hygiene is usually the cause of these problems.

Response: To prevent dental difficulties, you should clean your cat's teeth and gums regularly. First, stroke the pet's head, cheeks, and lips, to accustom him to being handled on that part of his body. Then put a small amount of cat toothpaste (available in pet stores and from vets) on your finger and rub it into the gums. The cat should like the flavor.

Then advance to the applicator (or a cat toothbrush, which can be obtained in the pet store, at a cat show, or from your vet). With the applicator, you'll be able to remove plaque from the teeth and massage the gums. The procedure should be done at least once a day. Calculus, or tartar, which is a hard accumulation of plaque, will have to be removed by the vet.

You should have your cat's teeth cleaned professionally by your vet at least once a year.

#10: FELINE IMMUNODEFICIENCY VIRUS (FIV)

Symptoms: Also known as feline AIDS, this fatal disease can be indicated by the presence of other illnesses or unusually aggressive behavior.

Cause: FIV is caused by a virus that was discovered in 1986. Similar to leukemia, it attacks the cat's immune system, and at this time no cure is known. The virus is picked up through contact and fighting with infected cats.

Response: Although there is no known transmission between cats and people, it's best to keep the animal indoors, away from direct contact with other humans or animals. Your vet should be contacted immediately if you think your pet has this problem.

#11: SKIN DISEASES

Symptoms: The cat may be experiencing loss of hair, scales, crusts, lumps, bumps, redness of skin, or inflammation of any part of the body.

Cause: Parasites may be the cause, including fleas. The problem may also be due to bacterial or fungal infections.

Response: See "Fleas" entry. You can check for fleas by using a flea comb, which has very narrow teeth. Run it through the cat's coat, and you may be able to turn up flea dirt or even the fleas themselves. In any event you should check with your vet.

#12: RABIES

Symptoms: The cat will become quite aggressive, bite and scratch without provocation, and may foam at the mouth.

Cause: This deadly virus, which has no cure, is acquired through the bite, scratch, or saliva of an infected animal. The nervous system and the brain of the animal are affected, and the cat is essentially driven insane.

Response: Stay away from any animal that you suspect has rabies and call the local health authorities. This disease can be as deadly to humans as it is to animals. Rabies can be prevented by being sure that your cat has all the required rabies vaccinations.

#13: TOXOPLASMOSIS

Symptoms: There may be no signs or symptoms, or a wide variety may occur, such as diarrhea. The most common sign is small, seedlike particles in the cat's feces.

Cause: This disease is caused by a microscopic parasite that gets into the cat's body through infected, undercooked meat, such as pork. Or the cat may get it by eating a mouse or rat.

Response: Pregnant women must stay away from animals with toxoplasmosis because of the possibility that contact may produce birth defects or miscarriages. Your vet must prescribe treatment.

To prevent this disease and protect yourself from it, avoid handling cat feces, clean the litter box regularly, and take your cat in for regular medical checkups.

#14: CAT ACNE

Symptoms: The cat develops a rash or irritation under the chin.

Cause: The owner has failed to clean out the food bowl, which must be thoroughly washed after every meal.

Response: Wash the cat's bowl, and apply a little zinc oxide on the soreness.

#15: FELINE LEUKEMIA

Symptoms: Your pet may stop eating, lose weight, and seem listless.

Cause: Leukemia, which most often affects cats that go outdoors, is passed on through saliva, urine, or bites from an infected cat. Cats that stay alone at home aren't at significant risk.

Response: This disease, which is not too common, is nevertheless fatal for cats who get it—so it's important to have your cat checked *and* vaccinated annually with a new leukemia vaccine. The shot, which can first be given to a kitten at about nine to twelve weeks of age, doesn't help a cat who already has the disease.

1 6 : EXCESSIVE HUNGER

Symptoms: The cat may eat excessive amounts of food and either gain or lose weight.

Cause: If the cat eats too much and gains weight, it may have a hormone problem. If it loses weight, there may be a malfunction in the thyroid gland (a hyperactive thyroid).

Response: Call your vet.

1 7 : FAILURE TO EAT

Symptoms: The cat may turn its nose up at all food, seem listless, or just pick over the meal.

Cause: A variety of illnesses, such as viruses or fever, may cause a lack of hunger. Or the cat may just be a finicky eater.

Response: If there is an illness, the vet will have to treat the underlying problem, and then you can expect your cat's appetite to return.

If your cat is just a finicky eater, you'll have to try different types of cat food, or perhaps throw in some fish, such as mackerel, to spice up the meal. If this experimentation doesn't work, contact your vet.

1 8 : SPRAYING

Symptoms: Your cat may begin to urinate outside the litter box, in a variety of places around the house.

Cause: Cats are very territorial, and your pet may have started the spraying because he saw another animal outside the house and decided to establish his ownership. Or a feeling of stress, as may happen when company or a new pet arrives, may trigger the spraying. It's also possible that your cat has a urinary tract problem.

Response: Try to remove any source of stress—or wait until the occasion for the stress has passed. For example, it may take a week or so for your cat to get used to the presence of a new pet or baby.

Then reintroduce the cat to the litter box. In effect you'll have to do an abbreviated potty-training routine.

If this doesn't work, see your vet to check for possible illness.

1 9 : FELINE UROLOGICAL SYNDROME (FUS)

Symptoms: The cat may seem listless, depressed, or weak. Also, he may have blood in his urine, urinate frequently, or fail to use the litter box.

Cause: The canal through which the cat urinates becomes blocked through infection, stones, or congenital abnormalities. Fat cats are especially susceptible.

Response: The problem can sometimes be relieved by changing the diet, such as eliminating foods high in magnesium; ensuring the intake of regulated amounts of clear, fresh water; or taking other measures prescribed by your vet. It's important to bring the vet into this situation as soon as possible because a full bladder can rupture and cause death.

#20: FELINE INFECTIOUS PERITONITIS (FIP)

Symptoms: Your pet may not want to eat, appear listless, hide from you and others, or develop a large abdomen.

Cause: This infectious disease, which is passed from infected cat to cat, involves an infection and inflammation of the lining of inner body organs.

Response: Only a vet can make a definitive diagnosis because the symptoms of this rare disease are often similar to those of other conditions. The disease can be prevented through the FIP vaccine.

Geriatric Cat Complaints

The older cat, over eight or nine years of age, has special medical concerns. The owner must monitor his water and food intake closely to be sure he gets enough. An increase in thirst can signal the onset of diabetes, kidney problems, or thyroid disease. A lack of appetite may indicate the presence of a fever.

Changes in urination can also be signs of illness. For example, if your cat seems to be making exceptionally frequent trips to the litter box, he may have a urinary tract infection. Or difficulty with bowel movements can mean that he has swallowed something, such as a fur ball—a common occurrence in older cats.

Also, watch his eyes to see if there is any change in their color or clarity: Older cats often develop cataracts, a condition that is signaled by cloudiness of the lenses. Also, watch the older cat's gums for redness or other discoloration. Gum disease is common among geriatric cats.

The older cat's coat may be another signal of a medical concern. A loss of luster can indicate a change in health. Also, older cats may have trouble cleaning themselves, so the owner has to take up the slack. Nails have to be trimmed regularly because older cats are prone to infections around the nail beds.

Trips to the vet every six to twelve months are recommended for the older cat because of the likelihood of deterioration in health with age. You'll find that your vet has access to many sophisticated diagnostic tools, such as ultrasound and electrocardiograms, to keep your older cat in the best possible health.

How to Give Your Cat Medicine

Early in my relationship with Crudge, I learned to give him medication because he caught a cold! Giving a sick cat a pill or liquid medication is actually quite easy—so long as you go about it gently and systematically. Here's a proven technique:

- First, put the cat up on a table or countertop where you can work easily with him.
- Since he's probably not used to being in that position, provide some security by putting a towel around his legs and snuggling it up around his neck. Hold him gently. Remember, restraining a cat too much will provoke fear and resistance.
- With a pill in one hand, use the other hand to hold the nape of your cat's neck and point the cat's nose to the ceiling, put the pill in the mouth, and let it drop down into his throat. (You may have to apply gentle pressure to each side of the cat's back jaw bones to get him to open his mouth.) Immediately

blow in his face. That will encourage him to swallow.

- With liquid medication, point his head upward, but not as high as you did with the pill. Place a dropper with medication in it into the side of the cat's mouth. Squeeze it slightly so that only a little medication comes out of the dropper. This will give the cat time to swallow. Continue squeezing the dropper just a little until all of the medication is gone.

If you observe any of these signs in your cat, *call your vet.* Your vet has years of medical training and schooling. Your vet can recognize and diagnose things you will miss. When it comes to your cat's health, your vet should be your best friend!

How Much Is Your Cat's Health Worth?

First-class medical care for a pet can cost about as much as care for a human. How much should you pay for your pet's needs? That depends on how much you have to spend and the likelihood that extraordinary measures will bring your cat back to health.

Here are some of the possibilities, given the advanced state of current medical techniques:

- A seven-week treatment of chemotherapy and cobalt radiation cost $4,000 for one pet, according to a report in *The New York Times* (Sept. 17, 1990). The procedure ensured the animal would live for another year or so.

Otherwise, he would have died in just three or four months.

- Major surgery, involving the animal's heart or bones, can cost $1,500 to $4,000.
- Pacemakers can be put into pets for about $700 to regulate their heartbeats (a bargain compared with human pacemakers, which typically cost more than $10,000 to implant, but still expensive).
- Surgeons, for varying fees, can repair heart valves, operate on the brain, and perform bone transplants.
- Some cats have been placed on dialysis machines to keep their kidneys functioning while they overcome serious infections.

It's been argued that such high costs and the use of sophisticated machines and procedures should be reserved for humans and not wasted on animals. But there is a growing perception that pets are often more important to their owners' well-being than non-pet-owners may realize. In fact, according to one study, more than two thirds of Americans regard their pets as members of the family, and one out of five actually see them as important a being as a child!

Pets are increasingly being accepted as important components in therapy for people who are elderly, sick, or emotionally needy. Spending a significant amount of money to improve the pet's health and prolong its life may in the long run be as important as treating the human owner.

Your best health strategy for your cat is **prevention.** Keep her well groomed, and if she is old, be sure she can remove waste material from her body. Clean her dishes and other eating equipment after every meal, and clean

out the litter box daily. Put in new litter at least once a
week. (Use gloves when you're dealing with your pet's
toilet to reduce the chances that you'll contract a disease
or infection.)

Also, pay close attention to having your cat eat well
and exercise adequately. In the last analysis, maintaining
cat health isn't that much different from maintaining
human health. An ounce of prevention is indeed worth a
pound of cure.

CHAPTER EIGHT

CAT-PROOFING YOUR HOME

JUST AS A PARENT MUST "CHILD-PROOF" a home to prevent toddlers from getting into things that could seriously hurt them, a cat owner must "cat-proof" his dwelling. The first step is to set up certain cat-control features in your home and be sure they work in protecting your cat. If you don't, you could be very sorry—as one man intent on impressing his girlfriend almost was.

Don's Near Disaster   Don had fallen deeply in love with Joan, and from their first date, he knew this was the woman he wanted to marry. But to seal the relationship, he had to prove himself to Joan's two cats, Tulip and Tom.

Tulip, a female, was fairly easy to get along with, but Tom was another matter. He was frisky and mischievous, and Don had noticed that he seemed fascinated by the world outside his mistress's home.

Unfortunately Tom's future in the great outdoors was not bright because he had been declawed—a procedure, as you know, I don't recommend. Due to his clawless state, Joan always left stern instructions, whenever anyone else was in charge of him, that he *had* to be kept inside. Otherwise he might hurt himself trying to climb or fight in the cold, cruel world. As it happened, Joan lived in a neighborhood filled with big, tough cats. She knew this particular cat-control policy was essential to the health and safety of her pets.

One day Joan had to go out for a while, and she asked Don to watch over her cats. He readily agreed because he had found the animals reasonably easy to handle when Joan was around. Besides, he had grown up with a couple of dogs, and that experience gave him an added degree of confidence.

But Don soon found that cats were a different brand of beast. He went out into Joan's backyard after she had left to do some chores, and as he moved back and forth, the sliding screen door periodically had to be opened. Tom, a crafty creature, lay in wait, watching for his big chance. He obviously was monitoring the opening and shutting of the door and gauging the possibility of escape.

Finally, when Don's hands were full of material he was carrying indoors, Tom bolted outside as the door opened. All Don saw was a black blur. In one smooth, continuous feline motion, Tom was out of the house and over the backyard fence. He jumped the entire six feet in a single bound!

The disaster had happened quickly, but it sank in more slowly. "I'm a dead man," Don finally muttered to himself. "I'm an idiot. I let that cat lull me and then make a fool of me."

The next thought that came to mind was, "Run out and intercept that cat from the front of the house!"

So Don flew out the front door—and nearly bowled over Joan, who was just arriving back home.

"What's happening?" she asked.

"Tom's out," Don answered, not stopping except to note the sick look that settled on Joan's face.

Then the rage arose: "If anything happens to my cat . . . !" she screamed after him, not finishing the threat. But Don could imagine what was in store for him if he didn't recover Tom.

Of course Don didn't see anything of the cat when he got outside, but he felt he had to make an attempt to find the animal. He scoured the neighborhood, looking under cars, searching behind bushes, and interrogating anyone he could find on the street, but all to no avail.

Crestfallen, he returned to face the music. He was going over in his mind what he would say to Joan. What could he promise—maybe to stand on nails for a few minutes every day for the rest of his life as penance? He couldn't imagine how he could get her forgiveness for such a transgression.

Don couldn't bear to go back in through the front door, so he walked around to the back. And what did he see when he reached the back? That cat, Tom, was sitting there looking out of the back screen door with a kind of smile.

Fortunately Don's near-disaster with Tom came out all right. But some owners have encountered *real* disasters when they fail to control their cat's environment effectively.

Does Your Household Harbor Any Hazards?

To cat-proof your home intelligently, you need a strategy. Most people who deal with hazards around the home on a stopgap or *ad hoc* basis usually find that they've forgotten some key danger area—and they learn about their oversight only after their pet has been hurt or threatened.

To assist you in developing your own comprehensive cat-proofing strategy, I've devised the following checklist that should apply to the environment of most cats. Look over these hazards first, and you'll be in a stronger position to design your own personal approach to making your home safe for your pet.

Dangerous Cat Toys   A great deal has been written about how certain toys or household items that seem like toys can be dangerous for children. For example, a small child may choke on a little soldier or suffocate by placing a plastic bag over his head. Consequently parents have to examine their floors, shelves, and other accessible areas closely to be sure that potentially dangerous items are out of reach.

Similarly the cat's environment must be cleared of dangerous "toys" or tempting items that may cause the pet harm or death. But owners have to be even more careful with cats because the animals are able to climb up onto areas that a small child would not be able to reach.

Some things owners should watch for include the following:

- Yarn, rubber bands, coins, or strings, which the cat may swallow. Vomiting may signal the problem. Surgery may be required to remove the object.

- Rubber or plastic balls or similar objects that the cat can chew up and swallow.
- Excessive hair on the cat or in the cat's living area, which may be swallowed and obstruct the digestive tract.
- Dead birds, mice, insects, or other animals that the cat may play with and swallow. The digestive tract may be blocked, or the cat may become sick from an infected animal.
- Pins, needles, or other sharp objects.
- Any small item that is shiny or appears otherwise interesting to the cat.

Chemicals and Cleaners   Anything that is poisonous for a human will be poisonous for a cat. Be sure not to leave cleaning fluids or other chemicals in a spot that may be accessible to the cat.

Antifreeze, in particular, tastes sweet to a cat. But when swallowed, it's lethal. An estimated nine out of ten cats who drink antifreeze die.

Plants   Many common household plants are potentially poisonous. For example, rhododendron, English ivy, and dumb cane, when eaten, can causing swelling of the throat. Other plants may lead to other types of poisoning, or may even kill the cat. The accompanying list of potentially toxic plants, with their poisonous parts, will provide you with more detailed guidelines.

Prescription and Over-the-Counter Drugs   No sleeping pills, cold medicine, tranquilizers, antibiotics, or other drugs should be kept in the reach of a cat. All medicine cabinets should be securely shut, and if you have a particularly active, inquisitive cat who likes to hop up on shelves and open doors and drawers, you'll have to place a clamp or lock on the door.

Don't take any chances! If you think your pet *may* get into your medicines, lock them up!

Illegal Drugs   Cats can become sick or die from many of the illegal drugs, such as cocaine. Marijuana can cause vomiting and diarrhea.

Holiday Decorations   Many people assume that the festive, happy atmosphere surrounding Christmas and other holidays somehow makes them immune to a pet tragedy. Actually the colorful, shiny decorations on a tree or in other parts of the house can provide an irresistible temptation to a cat. So keep ribbons, tinsel, small lights, and other such items away from your cat. Mistletoe, by the way, can cause nausea and vomiting.

Unsecured Doors and Screens   Remember the experience of the cat Tom at the beginning of this chapter. Indoor cats are often looking for a chance to get outside. But they aren't experienced in dealing with animals and situations in the great outdoors, and they may get into trouble before they realize what has happened. Fights or other contacts with stray cats are one of the greatest sources of feline leukemia and other diseases. Furthermore, if the cat has been declawed, as Tom was, the risks of injury increase immeasurably.

So be sure that you don't have any holes or rips in the screens around your house, and be certain that your doors are securely closed when you go in and out. If your cat is savvy enough to know how to unlatch a door, you will also have to *lock* your doors after you use them.

Unattended Children   Small children should not be

left alone with a cat, especially if the child is a visitor. The feline temperament doesn't take well to aggressive behavior on the part of a little human, and the response to pulling hair or other rough play may be a painful and damaging bite or swipe with the claws.

Other Pets in the House, Especially Dogs   No matter how well you think your dog and cat get along together, always prepare for the worst. Assume that your dog may become provoked or mischievous and try to attack the cat or vice versa. To counter this possibility, the cat should always be provided with one or more means of escape, such as a high shelf he can use as a haven, out of the dog's reach.

Unsecured Rides in Vehicles   Do *not* take your cat for a ride in your car without placing him in a regular cat carrying case. If you just put your cat unsecured in the backseat, he'll most likely jump around and interfere with your driving, and he may even hop out of the moving car.

Also, never take a cat for a ride in an unsecured manner in the back of a pickup truck. He'll probably jump out if no one is holding on to him, and even if he's being held in a person's lap, he may become excited and break loose.

Table Scraps or Unattended Food   Keep all human food away from your cat, unless you plan to use a few morsels of mackerel or some other tempting dish to entice your pet to eat his regular meal. Leaving food out where the cat can get to it will interfere with your own meal options and will also encourage the cat to eat the wrong kinds of things. Remember, commercially prepared cat foods are the best diet for your pet.

Open Windows in Upper Stories   One of the greatest causes of death for cats in New York City is that they fall from the windows of high buildings.

Some cat observers have noted that more deaths seem to occur during falls from second- and third-floor windows than from some higher floors. The reason for this may be that the tumbling cat has more of a chance to stabilize himself and land on his feet from a higher distance.

Even if this is true, there has to be a height ceiling above which most, if not all, cats will die if they fall. I wouldn't try to determine that ceiling and I wouldn't take any chances. Keep a screen on your upper windows or keep them securely closed to protect your pet.

These are just a few hazards and conditions that can harm your feline friend. Undoubtedly you can think of others that fit your particular environment. For example, if your cat has been declawed, you should be especially watchful for tempting high places, such as shelves or trees in your backyard, that may cause your cat to climb and fall.

Now, to encourage you to think more specifically about your own situation, move on to the next section, which involves fitting the above hazards and any others you can think of into a comprehensive personal plan to protect your cat from danger.

Designing Your Personal Cat-Proofing Strategy

Using the following plan, note the possible cat hazards in your environment and indicate what you can do about them. Check in the appropriate spot when you have cat-proofed a particular area.

Hazard	What to Do	Hazard Corrected
Dangerous cat toys:		
Chemicals and cleaners:		
Poisonous plants:		

Hazard	What to Do	Hazard Corrected
Prescription/ over-the-counter drugs:		
Illegal drugs:		
Holiday decorations:		

Hazard	What to Do	Hazard Corrected
Unsecured doors/screens:		
Unattended children:		
Other pets, especially dogs:		
Unsecured rides in vehicles:		

Hazard	What to Do	Hazard Corrected
Table scraps or unattended food:		
Open windows in upper stories:		
Other hazards:		

Now that you've established your plan, put it into effect. When you correct a hazard, place a check in the "Hazard Corrected" column. Or when another problem comes to mind, add it to the "Other Hazards" list and take care of it. After all the hazards in your home have been dealt with, you can feel more secure that your pet really is quite safe in the environment you've created for him.

Common Poisonous Plants

Plant	Toxic Parts	Plant Type
Aconite	roots, foliage, seeds	garden flower
Apple	seeds	cultivated tree
Arrowgrasses	leaves	marsh plants
Atropa belladonna	entire plant esp. seeds, roots	garden herb
Autumn crocus	entire plant	garden flower
Azaleas	entire plant	cultivated & wild shrub
Baneberry	berries, roots	wildflower
Bird-of-paradise	pods	garden flower
Black Locust	entire plant esp. bark, shoots	tree
Bloodroot	entire plant esp. stem, roots	wildflower, herb
Box	entire plant esp. leaves	ornamental shrub
Buckeye	sprouts, nuts, seeds	tree
Buttercup	entire plant esp. leaves	wildflower, garden herb
Caladium	entire plant	houseplant
Carolina jessamine	flowers, leaves	ornamental plant
Castor bean	entire plant esp. beans	houseplant
Chinaberry tree	berries	tree
Chokecherries	leaves, cherries, pit	wild shrub
Christmas berry	leaves	shrub
Christ rose	rootstock, leaves	garden
Common privet	leaves, berries	ornamental shrub
Corn cockle	seeds	wildflower, weed
Cowbane	entire plant esp. roots	wildflower, herb
Cow cockle	seeds	wildflower, weed
Cowslip	entire plant esp. leaves, stem	wildflower, herb
Daffodil	bulbs	garden flower
Daphne	bark, berries, leaves	ornamental shrub
Death camas	leaves, stems, seeds, flowers	field herb
Delphinium (larkspur)	entire plant esp. sprouts	wildflower
Dumb cane	entire plant	houseplant
Dutchman's breeches	roots, foliage	wild & garden flower
Elderberry	leaves, bark, roots, buds	tree
Elephant's ear	entire plant	houseplant
English ivy	entire plant esp. leaves, berries	ornamental vine

European bittersweet	entire plant esp. berries	vine
False flax	seeds	wild herb
False hellebore	roots, leaves, seeds	ornamental flower
Fan weed	seeds	wildflower, herb
Field peppergrass	seeds	wildflower, herb
Flax	seedpods	wildflower, herb
Foxglove	leaves	wild & garden flower
Holly	berries	shrub
Horsechestnut	nuts, sprouts	tree
Horse nettle	entire plant esp. berries	wildflower, herb
Hyacinth	bulbs	wild & houseplant
Iris	leaves, roots	wild & garden flower

SOURCE: Cat Fanciers' Association.

Common Poisonous Plants

Plant	Toxic Parts	Plant Type
Jack-in-the-pulpit	entire plant esp. roots, leaves	wildflower
Jatropha	seeds	tree, shrub
Jerusalem cherry	unripe fruit, foliage	ornamental plant
Jimsonweed	entire plant esp. seeds	field plant
Laburnum	seeds, pods, flowers	ornamental plant
Lantana	foliage	houseplant
Larkspur	young plants	wildflower
Laurels	leaves	shrub
Lily of the valley	leaves, flowers	garden & wildflower
Lupines	seeds, pods	shrub
Manchineel tree	sap, fruit	tree
Matrimony vine	leaves, shoots	ornamental vine
Mayapple	unripe fruit, roots, foliage	wildflower
Milk vetch	entire plant	wildflower
Mistletoe	berries	houseplant
Monkshood	entire plant esp. roots, seeds	wildflower
Moonseed	fruit, roots	vine
Morning glory	seeds, roots	wildflower
Mountain mahogany	leaves	shrub
Mustards	seeds	garden flower
Narcissus	bulbs	garden flower
Nicotiana	leaves	garden flower
Nightshade	leaves, berries	wildflower, vine
Oaks	shoots, leaves	tree
Oleander	leaves	ornamental shrub
Philodendrons	entire plant	houseplant
Pokeweed	roots, seeds, berries	field plant
Poinsettia	leaves, stems, flowers	houseplant
Poison hemlock	leaves, stems, fruit	field plant
Potato	shoots, sprouts,	garden plant
Rattle box	entire plant	wildflower

Common Poisonous Plants

Plant	Toxic Parts	Plant Type
Rhododendron	leaves	ornamental shrub
Rhubarb	leaves	garden plant
Rosary pea	seeds	houseplant
Skunk cabbage	entire plant esp. roots, leaves	marshplant
Smartweed	sap	wildflower
Snow-on-the-mountain	sap	field plant
Sorghum	leaves	grass
Star of Bethlehem	entire plant	wildflower
Velvet grass	leaves	grass
Wild black cherry	leaves, pits	tree
Wild radish	seeds	wildflower
Wisteria	pods, seeds	ornamental plant
Woody aster	entire plant	wildflower
Yellow jessamine	entire plant	ornamental vine
Yellow oleander	entire plant esp. leaves	garden plant
Yellow pine flax	entire plant esp. seedpods	wildflower
Yew	bark, leaves, seeds	ornamental tree

SOURCE: Cat Fanciers' Association.

CHAPTER NINE

CAT PARA-PHERNALIA

To be a *complete* cat owner, you must become aware of the variety of cat paraphernalia that is available to make your life easier. In particular you need to educate yourself about the availability of cat services, such as cat-sitting or professional grooming, and also about the pros and cons of different types of cat equipment.

What Cat Services Are Available?

I've already mentioned a number of services that are available to you as a pet owner. The first and most important is medical service. That is, you *must* contact a veterinarian when you bring your cat home and then stay in touch for regular annual checkups.

In addition, there are many optional services that you may want to use. Here are a few possibilities:

- Professional groomers. Many owners hire professional groomers when their cat's coat gets in such a state of disarray that they can't do a proper job on it at home.
- Cat trainers. Having trouble teaching your cat to sit or heel? Check the "Pet and Dog Training" entry in your yellow pages. Also, your local pet store, cat shows, and animal shelters are all great resources to find a cat trainer.
- Pet cemeteries and crematories. Again, check the yellow pages.
- Pet exercising services. The yellow pages will provide you with names and numbers.
- Pet supplies and food stores.
- Cat-sitters. Always get references.

How can you find out about the availability of these services in your area? As I've indicated above, many larger cities list these services in the yellow pages of the telephone book. But even before you open the phone book, perhaps the best first step is to contact trusted friends and acquaintances who may know about the service you want. Your vet's office, cat shows, friends with pets, and the local pet supply shop are excellent starting points.

As for cat-sitters, the last item on the above list, more needs to be said.

Should You Hire a Cat-Sitter?

This is almost like asking, "Should you hire a baby-sitter?" The answer is a resounding *yes* unless you want to be tied down to your house or apartment for the rest of your life.

How can you find a sitter and what are some of the qualifications you should look for? This question is best answered first by considering the experiences of Patti J. Moran, who has opened some new territory on the frontier of pet-sitting.

Moran was laid off from her job a number of years ago, and as a result she literally went to the dogs—and cats and gerbils and birds. Instead of trying to find another employer, she went into business for herself in Winston-Salem, North Carolina, with a pet-sitting firm she called "Crazy 'Bout Critters."

Now Moran employs more then thirty-five part-time pet-sitters and other workers—*and* she has founded the National Association of Pet Sitters (NAPS). NAPS has established professional standards and job networks for hundreds of pet-sitting members around the country.

If you need a sitter to stay with your cat while you're out or on a trip, you may be able to find a suitable person among your friends or by referral from other pet owners. Or you could contact the National Association of Pet Sitters at 632 Holly Avenue, Winston-Salem, North Carolina 17101. The organization's telephone number is (919) 723-PETS.

Before you hire any pet-sitter, get references and check them out!

What Sort of Equipment Does Your Cat Need?

At a minimum every cat owner should have the following items, which can be purchased in most pet stores and at cat shows. *Note:* I've sometimes mentioned manufacturers and other suppliers and service organizations here and elsewhere in the book, but these references are included only for illustrative and informational purposes. They shouldn't be taken as endorsements. Check them out and make up your own mind.

- A cat comb and brush

     Remember, those with wide-set teeth are best for cats such as Persians, which have a lot of hair. Brushes are best for removing excess hair and preventing the possibility of fur balls, which the cat may swallow. Combs are a good alternative and are essential for checking your cat for fleas.

- A cat-grooming glove

     It's best to select one specifically made for cats and available through pet stores. The advantage of a glove is that it gives you another alternative to a brush and also provides an opportunity for hand-to-cat contact. This will help you develop a closer relationship with your cat.

- A carrying case

     You may want two of these, one designed for airplane and other public-transportation travel, and another for auto transport. The first will be constructed in a sturdier fashion than the second.

- Nail clippers

     A variety are available specifically for cat use and are sold at any cat store. One set of clippers is all you need. Just select a sturdy pair that fits your hands comfortably. Remember, clipping those claws is essential if you hope to minimize the damage to furniture, drapes, and clothing that can be caused by an indoor cat.

- Tweezers

  I recommend that every owner keep a set of tick tweezers handy, just in case they are needed for the pet. The Safari Tick Tweezer is a special type with a tip that can be heated before use. The heat encourages the tick to release its grip on the cat's skin. Information is available at Whitco Manufacturing Inc., 2501 Middle Country Road, Centereach, New York 11720. Telephone: (516) 981-4545.

- Cat collars

  Every cat should have a collar and wear the collar always—indoors and out. The collar should have an elastic component, so that the cat can get out of it if it is snared on an item in your home or on a tree branch. Also, the collar should include an identification tag with the cat's name, owner's name, address, phone number, and vaccination information.

- Harness and leash

  Owners who like to take their cats out for walks or runs should get a cat harness and leash. (Some harnesses have a leash attached.) The harness should fit over the cat's front legs and chest, not just over the neck. Also, the leash should be long enough to allow the cat and owner some freedom of movement. Do *not* remove the collar when the cat is wearing its harness.

- Eating and drinking equipment

  Every cat needs a plate and water pan, and there are currently some quite sophisticated ones on the market. For example, the Van Ness company's Kit 'N Kaboodle in-

cludes a cat pan that comes color-coordinated
in mauve or blue; a double dish for food (in
case you serve your pet two courses); and a
water dish. In addition, this combination
deal offers a litter pan and a pack of liners
for the pan.

- Litter gear

    Obviously your cat will need a litter box
or pan. It's best to buy one at your pet store
so that you're sure to have the right depth
and protection from leakage. If you don't
know what size litter pan to purchase for
your cat, take your cat with you to the pet
store and place your cat in different pans
until you find the right size. Most pet stores
won't mind this.

    Get a disposal bag, such as those provided
by Van Ness or Auto Kitty. This addition will
make clean-up much easier. Another type of
disposal bag is the ordinary large trash bag.
Place the litter pan inside the bag. Then, fill
the bag with litter. When the litter is soiled
and ready to change, simply close the bag with
the soiled litter in it and place it in the trash.

    Litter can be purchased from pet or grocery
stores. Usually it's a claylike substance and
may be processed so that it absorbs and combines cat urine and feces quite effectively. Ever
Clean cat litter, for example, comes in several
types, which are designed for multiple cat use,
single cat use, or a heavy-duty type for cats
that like to dig or scratch. The litter is treated
so that it minimizes odor and can usually be
disposed of in the toilet (though some heavy-
duty types can't be flushed). Another clumping

litter you can purchase at the grocery store is
Tidy Scoop. As I stated before, I don't recco-
mend flushing any litter.

- A ready supply of cat food

  By now you probably realize that cats
should eat commercially prepared cat food,
not human food. This way they'll be sure to
get a sufficient balance of necessary nutrients
to maintain good health. In contrast, feeding
them with scraps from the table may give
them too much fat and lead to obesity, or
otherwise upset their diets. Some manufacturers, such as Tami, IAMS, and Ralston
Purina, offer separate formulas for adult cats
and kittens. The kitten food includes a
higher percentage of protein.

  Generally speaking, the nutrients in commercially prepared cat food break down this
way:

- 14–32 percent protein
- 20 percent fat
- 3–4 percent fiber
- Less than 6.5 percent ash

Other possibilities for special cat equipment include
special pooper-scoopers and mats for cat use. Such items
are supplied by companies like Cosmic Pet Products, 133
South Burhans Boulevard, Hagerstown, Maryland 21740.
Telephone: (301) 797-3115.

  Also, you'll want to consider the following additional
items:

- Catnip. This herb is quite helpful if you're
  trying to train or reward your cat.

- Cat toys, such as fake mice, balls, and other
  items. (Make sure these toys are safe toys.)
- Scratching post, to keep your cat's nails dull
  and provide needed exercise.
- Cat sweaters, for pets who like to spend
  time outside with you in cold weather.
- Bells. These should be attached to a collar
  when the cat goes outdoors to warn off birds
  or other animals that you don't want your
  cat to attack or kill.

A Word About Bells

One morning I decided I wanted another cup of coffee. In
order to get it, I had to walk through the dining room and
into the kitchen. As I walked through the dining room,
something caught my eye, but I ignored it. Once I was in
the kitchen something else caught my eye, and this time
I looked. The "something" was a small gray feather. As a
matter of fact, there were several somethings, and they
were gray feathers of varying sizes.

Cautiously, I walked into the dining room and looked
at the spot were the first flutter had caught my eye. To my
dismay there were dozens of silver-gray feathers in the
corner of the room, but no source. Carefully (not wanting
to distress myself), I bent down and peeked behind the
telephone table, which is by a large silk plant. Sure enough,
Crudge, secure in his hiding place, was ferociously chew-
ing on what had once been a bird. (At least he had the
decency to eat the bird in the dining room!) Feathers were
everywhere!

Crudge, happy for killing his prey, was in heaven. I
was not. The bird was quite dead and nearly gone.

It was a pretty sure bet that Crudge had gotten the bird

out of my garden. I found myself in a bit of a quandary. Crudge likes to go outside. I have a birdbath because I enjoy the beauty of wild birds. Result: By owning a cat that also enjoys frolicking in the garden, I was practically enticing these little wonders of nature to meet an early death. But I knew what to do.

As Crudge chomped away on the bird, I ran upstairs and began going through my Christmas decorations. I knew I had a bell somewhere, but where? Finally, I found several and chose the bell that made the loudest sound. Quickly, I ran downstairs and waited until Crudge walked away from his prey. At that point I enticed my kitten to come to me, took off his collar, added the bell, and put the collar back on.

That was several weeks ago. The bell must be working because Crudge hasn't brought any more live food into the house to eat. Of course, you can hear the bell whenever he jumps or runs. It's not very loud, but it is loud enough to scare the birds away.

By the way, apparently the bird was too rich for Crudge, because six hours later he threw the whole thing up. This is not my favorite memory, but I certainly did learn an excellent lesson. If you want to continue to enjoy live birds in your garden, cats must wear bells on their collars.

Of course there are many other possibilities for useful items that you may buy or make for your cat. But the above suggestions should prepare you for most of your cat's needs or emergencies. Try to keep all your cat supplies in one place so that you can take inventory periodically and see what you need to buy the next time you go to the store. That way you'll be sure to keep your cat as happy and comfortable as you are.

CHAPTER TEN

CATS ARE PEOPLE TOO

CATS ARE MARVELOUS COMPANIONS. That's why they are the most popular pet in America, with nearly 60 million now living in homes across the land.

Why are people so drawn to cats? The simple reason is that in many, many ways cats are *like* humans. They enjoy being appreciated, loved, and cuddled. Yet at the same time they like their comforts, their independence, and their privacy.

There are differences of course. Unlike humans, cats are said to require on average about eighteen hours of sleep a day. (So if your cat seems irritable or short-tempered, maybe she's not getting her full beauty rest. Of course she may be trying to tell you something else, such as that she's ill.) Furthermore a cat's hearing is typically five times as good as a human's, and they are five times as capable at seeing in the dark as we are, according to cat aficionado Desmond Morris. The cat's whiskers, by the way, are used to help them feel their way through the dark to the presence of prey, which they may feel with the whiskers before they jump in for the kill.

Their "Human" Status   Still, even with these differences, cats are a lot like us. Specifically, domestic cats resemble young people when we take over their care.

To be sure, stray cats have demonstrated quite clearly that they can take care of themselves, but if you assume responsibility for a cat—if you take her into your home and condition her to become a member of your family—you in effect place that cat in a status similar to that of your child. You have to feed her, watch over her health, and be sure that her safety isn't jeopardized if she goes outside the environment you've created for her.

The status of cats as almost-but-not-quite human can place interesting demands on an owner. Fortunately, though, most cats are natural survivors, as is shown in the experience of former diplomat Peggy Miller.

To Russia with Love

Peg's two cats, Humbert and K-Woo, were Siamese—and they were both quite large. Humbert weighed fifteen pounds, and K-Woo wasn't far behind. They both had extremely thick, long fur, and both were trained to walk with a leash (though Humbert always needed plenty of loud correction to keep him in line).

Some Serious Feline Figuring   When Peg received orders to go to Moscow, she felt prepared because her cats were well trained, healthy, and widely traveled. But she got an inkling of the adventures ahead when she went to a State Department briefing and learned that even though animals were allowed in Russia, taking them there while on assignment was discouraged.

The reasons for the negative response? There were no vets in Russia. No cat food. No cat sand. In fact, there wasn't even much toilet paper for humans. Furthermore Peg was given a limited weight allowance, and because food and supplies were scarce in Russia, the diplomatic corps was encouraged to bring enough food and laundry soap to last two years.

So Peg went home, pulled out her calculator, and figured what she could delete from her luggage to enable her to bring her cats. She decided she could do without so much food, but toilet paper was another matter. She tried to think how much toilet paper one person would use in a month times twenty-four—and by the way, how much would that weigh? Peg also knew that she had to bring extra soap, toothpaste, and shampoo for herself. Most other items in her luggage were negotiable.

She then moved on to her pets. Cat food was a big concern because she figured it would take 730 six-ounce cans to last the cats during their stay. In a massive understatement she suggested to a friend that this item might push her over her weight limit. When she began to consider cat sand, she finally knew she was in *deep* trouble.

Clearly some radical surgery had to be performed on her cats' luggage. So the first thing she eliminated was the cat sand. Then she reduced the amount of cat food to two months' worth. Otherwise she would have had to eliminate her own toilet paper and laundry soap.

With the weight situation finally settled, Peg confronted a second problem. It seemed that all the supplies she was sending over would have to be shipped by boat.

That meant she and the cats couldn't expect to see any of it for about two months. She was supposed to bring only clothes on her flight over to Moscow, with no food, supplies—and certainly no cat sand!

As a solution Peg decided that she would have to wait until she reached Russia to deal with the cats' diet those first couple of months. She already knew that the only logical answer was to have them eat human food for a while.

A Trying Trip   Finally Peg left for Moscow. She stayed over in New York at the Plaza Hotel before her flight left and reserved a suite for herself and the two cats. The Plaza had assured her that the cats would be welcome, but there was a moment of hesitation in the lobby when Humbert began to howl from his carrying case.

"Ma'am, perhaps your cat would be happier if you took him out of his carrier," the manager suggested.

Peg complied, hooked a leash on each cat, and watched in amazement as Humbert immediately quieted down. Both cats lifted their tails—a confident, "follow-me" sign—and walked into the elevator in satisfied silence, to the applause of other guests waiting in the Plaza lobby.

As a kind of going-away gift for the cats, Peg bought each a flashy, jewel-studded collar. Humbert's was black leather with three rows of white rhinestones and K-Woo's was red with two rows of red rhinestones. This sort of apparel may seem extravagant for a cat, but after all, Peg and the Siamese were "related by adoption." Also, as it happened, the classy look of the cats helped get them through customs.

At the airport in Moscow Peggy was met by an officious government physician, who demanded papers for the cats. It seemed that nothing she could offer him was acceptable. Meanwhile the baggage carrier dropped the airline cat cage at the doctor's feet—and Humbert began to vocalize.

"*Otkroite!*" the doctor ordered. Translation: "Open!" Peggy opened the cage, and out stepped the two Siamese. The doctor's eyes grew enormous. "Oh, *bolshia capitolisti!*" he exclaimed. Translation: "Big capitalists!"

Those fat cats, wearing their flashy collars, apparently convinced him he was dealing with felines of some means. So he waved them through with no further problems.

The Life of a Feline Diplomat   The next few months were great for the cats. Peg's Russian maid, Nadia, taught K-Woo a few Russian commands and worked out an agreement with them about their food. The canned cat food, when it finally arrived, only supplied the cats for about two months. Nadia began to shop on the black market and prepared home-cooked meals of liver and fish, both lightly salted and spiced.

Needless to say, the cats completely lost their taste for regular commercial fare. When they returned to Washington two years later, both went on a hunger strike for two weeks and in the process lost a considerable amount of weight.

Peg entertained a great deal in the embassy, with a constant train of dignitaries going in and out of the quarters. One of the most popular events was showing American movies. For some reason *Jaws* was always a great icebreaker.

But there was a side show that also went on during the films. For some unknown reason a particularly large colony of mice roamed around in the American embassy. Humbert discovered that the best hunting time was the period when the lights were out for the movies. More than once he deposited a not-very-dead mouse at the foot of some unsuspecting diplomat.

Peg left Moscow for personal reasons before her tour of duty was up, and she had to leave Humbert and K-Woo in the care of Nadia in the American embassy in Moscow. After she had arrived back in Washington, Peg picked up the *Washington Post* one morning and was shocked to see her Moscow residence on fire! She immediately called the State Department and asked for a patch into Moscow, but her request was denied because only one line was available.

"I don't care if you have *no* lines," Peg replied. "I have two cats in the north wing of the American embassy, and I'm going to get through. I'll call the president." Finally after four hours of pressing the issue she got some satisfaction. "Please don't call us anymore," the official said. "We'll call you back." True to their word, the State Department called her that afternoon with this message: "Humbert and K-Woo are alive and well, rescued by the chargé d'affaires."

Both cats were flown back to the States first-class, each with his own seat. According to the airline, they were fed Beluga caviar and assorted hors d'oeuvres.

Such is the life of the feline diplomat.

Can Cats Really Communicate?

Can a cat owner really "talk" to a cat, or is such interaction actually nothing more than feline-inspired fantasy?

Cat Talk   A number of experts have studied the body language and sounds of cats in an effort to identify messages that the cat may be trying to convey. Here are a few that have been noted by Dr. Michael Fox, an author, veterinarian, syndicated columnist, and cat expert:

- Half-closed eyes indicate relaxation.
- A vertical tail is a signal that says, "I'm coming," or "Follow me." This is exactly the message conveyed by Peggy Miller's cats in the Plaza Hotel.
- Leaning and drooling indicate contentment and regression to a kittenish state, especially when the signs occur as the cat is being petted.
- Crouching down in an attempt to become smaller can be a sign of fear, submission or attack.
- Hair standing up, and generally appearing puffed up, can display anger and an attitude of power toward an adversary.
- When a cat raises her back—bares her teeth, and fusses at you—leave the cat alone. She doesn't want to be bothered and is showing you by her "frightening" behavior. Even though silent, the message is loud and clear.

Communication Between Animals

My dog, Scruffette, eats more than any dog I have ever seen or heard of. It seems that Scruff is always on a diet. Among Scruff's favorite foods are carrots, apple cores, and broccoli. Scruff has also found a new food that she enjoys immensely—my cat Curmudgeon's food. And Crudge loves Scruff's diet food!

You can imagine the feeding schedule I have devised to keep these two apart. I even place Crudge's food up high so Scruff won't eat it. However, recently I observed an interesting standoff between the two animals. I was working in the kitchen and, by Crudge's insistent meows, decided it was time to feed the kitten. I placed Crudge's food on the floor, knowing that Scruff was sleeping in another part of the house. Crudge ate a little of his dinner and then flopped down on the kitchen floor about a foot away from his food. A few moments later Scruff arrived.

Still flat on the floor, Crudge just eyed Scruffette as though he was daring her to go for his food. Scruff stood very still, looked at the food, looked at me, then looked back at the food again. Scruff took a step forward. I told Scruff, "No." Crudge, still lying down, eyed Scruff.

Scruff took another step forward, eyed Crudge, eyed me, and eyed the food. Crudge stood slowly, as though he were going for a lazy walk, took two steps and stopped, not quite blocking his food and not quite blocking Scruff. This was Scruff's chance. She began her advance toward the food dish. I watched.

Scruff took about two steps. Crudge raised his back, bristled his fur, bared his teeth, and closed the gap between Scruff and himself. Scruff quickly got the message, stepped backward, and with her tail between her legs, left the kitchen. Crudge's food was untouched. These animals were communicating.

- Purring may be a sign of relaxation.

According to a joint study of cat communication conducted by experts at Tulane University in New Orleans and at the Museum Alexander Koenig in Bonn, Germany, however, purring may be a more complex phenomenon than we've always thought.

This investigation revealed that a purr, which is defined as a soft, buzzing sound, like a rolled *r*, is coordinated in the brain and produced by the voice box during inhaling and exhaling. Though there are consistencies in purring among cats regardless of age, sex, or size, the tones vary greatly in loudness and harmonics.

The experts making this report determined that the purr occurs both during times of contentment *and* during times of stress. Their conclusion: We really don't know the precise reason that a cat purrs.

Cat Therapy   Increasingly those working with the elderly, the sick, and the emotionally disturbed are finding that cats and other pets can help with therapy. The mood of the human who is placed in contact with the pet often improves dramatically.

One therapist told me that he had been trying to get pets for many of his patients because he found dramatic improvement with those who had an animal companion. One person who hadn't talked for years reportedly began talking when he was placed in contact with an animal.

Why are cats proving to be good therapy? There are several explanations:

- Cats are an antidote to loneliness.
    Because they make good companions, cats given to isolated elderly and sick people serve as "someone" to love and talk to. That can make a world of difference in improving the mood and combating depression.
- Cats give their owners a new purpose in life.
    When you become a cat owner, you immediately have to take responsibility for another living being. The animal's life and health depend directly on you. Those people who have been moping about, concerned only for themselves, now find that they have to care for someone else and organize their lives so that they are not the only focus.

- Cats are capable of establishing a real relationship with humans.

     One of the reasons that cat owners become so distraught when they lose a pet is that they have experienced an authentic form of communication and an exchange of true love with their pet. It's hard to quantify exactly what goes on in this interaction, but one thing is clear: There is a *real* relationship that is similar to the one that develops between humans.

The concept of the cat as an instrument of therapy is quite new. In fact we were the first national television show to break the story of pets as therapy nearly eleven years ago, and the broad implications of the idea have been unfolding ever since in hospitals, prisons, institutions for the mentally ill, and nursing homes around the country.

So never sell a cat short! Their potential for establishing rich relationsips with humans is still being explored. It wouldn't surprise me if someday a cat doesn't set up his own feline personal-advice hot line to keep curious humans appraised of the latest cat-human developments!

CHAPTER ELEVEN

THE JOYS OF A PET JOURNAL

To get the most out of your experience with your cat, I suggest that you keep a pet journal. This daily record of thoughts, observations, and events should be recorded in a daily diary of the type you can buy in any stationery store. It's best to purchase one that is book size or larger and provides lined spaces to write on, with a separate page for each day's entries.

Here are a couple of recent entries from my own journal:

June 30, 1992

I think that Crudge had a field day last night. As I was sleeping, I heard a loud bang but was too tired to do anything about it. This morning I noticed that the curtain was missing from the window. As I walked down the hall to let Scruffette out, I noticed that the curtain was at the end of the hall. I don't know how it got there, but my guess is that Crudge had something to do with this. My cat's escapades really make me laugh!

July 14, 1992

I was sleeping. I usually am at 5:30 A.M. but on this particular morning Crudge started playing with the venetian blind in my bedroom. In my sleepy state, it sounded as though Crudge was batting the blind against the wall. Without opening my eyes, I said, "Hush, Crudge!" Smart cat that Crudge is, he stopped.

A few minutes later, *bang, bang* came slamming into my sleep once again. Again, without opening my eyes, I said, "Crudge, stop it! Now!" That "now" did it and that clever cat stopped.

A few minutes later, it happened again. I was not happy at this point and finally opened my eyes and yelled, "Crudge, knock it off!"

In the darkened room my eyes focused on the area the sound was coming from. It looked very strange. Crudge seemed to be standing on his toes and leaning against the blind. I dragged myself out of bed and walked to the blind. As I got closer it became very apparent the Crudge wasn't on his toes at all. The hook on his collar was caught on the blind, and he was hanging! I couldn't help myself. I started laughing as I rushed to unhook Crudge and made a mental note to change the S hook on Crudge's collar.

August 1, 1992

Cats are nocturnal. If you don't believe it, just get one or two cats as pets. Crudge and Scruff always seem to play, bark, and screech when the lights are out and I'm drifting off to sleep.

Last night as I slept, and for no apparent reason, Crudge

leapt on my face, keeping his claws in. You figure that one out!

In addition to a daily log, you can write poems about your cat. This poem about the neighborhood cat Unibar was written by one of our viewers, James David, who is a playwright.

I live in an apartment
I have a cat
or it has me.
This cat kind of adopts people who move into
these apartments.
It likes to hang around, I've noticed.
When I have a girlfriend over, this cat is right there,
hanging around,
checking up on the action, I guess.
No one's quite decided if this cat is
a boy or a girl cat,
no one really seems to care.
Anyway, I call it a "her."
This cat's name is Unibar.
Unibar has lived in my apartment building eleven years.
Longer than I have.
Longer than anyone else has lived around here,
I've noticed.
Unibar has twenty-eight toes,
more than me
or anyone else
that I know of.
One morning, I awoke on my couch to find
Unibar with her big paw right in my hand,
and the other day, she chased my heels all the way to
my door and into my kitchen.

It's rumored that several of today's movie stars used to live
in these apartments too,
but in my opinion,
they can't put a candle to old Unibar.

The pet journal will serve several functions:

- You'll be able to build a record of your cat's health, development, and individual characteristics that will enable you to get to know him better.
- You'll have a record of your feelings about your pet—and the way your relationship has developed. There can be tremendous satisfaction and joy in reading back over the times you've spent with your pet.
- You'll see both the ups *and* the downs of your interactions if you're honest and complete in your entries. Also, you should include an explanation of how you have resolved different problems. This way you'll be in a position to monitor yourself and avoid past mistakes in the future.
- Clippings or other outside memorabilia slipped in the journal's pages can remind you of important specific events relating to your pet, such as cat shows or trips you took together.

To give you a more comprehensive idea of what such a journal might look like, consider the following sample entries that record the life of a shelter cat named Kitty. The writer is a mother who had some experience with cats in her youth, and her daughter, Jenny, nine years old, is a first-time owner.

Kitty's Journal

YEAR ONE

January 13.   Today Jenny and I picked up the cutest little kitten from the local animal shelter. He was a frisky little tomcat, already neutered. Of all the kittens in his group, he was the first to run over and say hello to us. He seemed so excited and friendly that it was love at first sight for Jenny. We decided on the spot to bring the kitten home.

January 14.   Jenny and I argued for most of the day over what to name the kitten. I thought we should have a distinctive name like Blossom Street, which is where his first home, the animal shelter, is located. But Jenny is adamant just to call him Kitty. Our final compromise? Kitty.

January 15.   In line with our prior agreement, Jenny has started caring for Kitty by putting out several litter pans and feeding him. I certainly don't want to have the full responsibility—but we'll see how long this lasts. I don't know what I'll do if Jenny fails to meet her responsibilities.

January 17.   Kitty is adjusting nicely to his new home. He's as curious and active as he was in the shelter, and he appears to be in good health. Seems to be a fairly big cat for his age—about five weeks, with short, black-and-white coat, which will be easy to groom.

Also, I've called the vet for an examination in about two weeks. We figure that Kitty will be about seven weeks old at the time of the exam. The vet says that he'll be able to have rabies shots and other vaccinations beginning at that point.

January 25.   Jenny continues to uphold her end of the bargain. Amazing! Giving her responsibility for the cat gives her a sense of being more grown up. I've noticed she also seems more willing to do her homework on her own and otherwise take charge of her life. Maybe every nine-year-old should be required to take care of a pet!

January 31.   Kitty got a clean bill of health at his visit to the vet today. He also began his vaccinations, which will continue over the next few months. He didn't like being handled by the doctor, but it's necessary if we want to have a healthy cat!

At the vet's suggestion, we've decided against declawing. Although Kitty will be primarily a house cat, we want to give him the option of going outside every now and then. The doctor said he would be at risk of injury from climbing or fights with other animals if he lacks claws.

February 14.   Valentine's Day. We gave a "party" for Kitty to celebrate the first month he has spent with us. Jenny gave him a special valentine with a large, cute kitten on it. Kitty actually snuggled up to it and sniffed around, as though he expected the paper cat to come to life. I really wonder, though, if Kitty doesn't regard himself as a human, rather than a cat.

We also gave him some presents—some special balls

and a toy in the shape of a mouse. Are we encouraging his predatory instincts?

February 28.   Increasingly in the last few days Kitty has been scratching up our furniture. He ripped a hole in the sofa and was about to go after the drapes before I caught him.

His nails are obviously too long, but I'm leery of trying to cut them. Should I give the job to Jenny? Would it be too dangerous for her? How about calling in a professional groomer? That seems a cop-out, but I'll have to think about it.

March 1.   I decided to take the first stab at cutting the cat's claws. Jenny's too young for this, but I think it's a bad precedent, to call in an outsider. After all, this is a family matter!

I'm following instructions I received from the vet and also another cat owner I know. It wasn't easy. As I held Kitty's feet and tried to cut, he squirmed around so much that I couldn't hold him—he even took a swipe at me!

On calling my cat-owner friend, I learned I shouldn't restrain Kitty so much when I was cutting. It is scary, to start cutting without having a really firm hold on the cat, but I did it.

I held him in my lap, petted him, and gradually stroked my way down to his left front paw. Then I gently raised the paw in my hand, pressed down on the top of the claw so that the point of the nail protruded, and clipped. It worked! Even though I was afraid of cutting at the wrong place and hurting the cat, I managed to do it right.

Now I have some confidence. Cutting claws isn't really all that hard. But I think I'll let Jenny get a little older and develop some more experience caring for the cat before I allow her to try this. She seems happy enough to let me handle this particular job right now. Besides, I'm just learning myself!

April 5.   Kitty's first day outdoors. Perhaps we've been too cautious, but I wanted him to grow a little and get used to us before he tried this challenge.

Jenny put a harness and leash on him and encouraged him to run around the yard with her. Kitty even tried to scale a couple of low trees. He's especially interested in the birds that were flying about the yard and landing on the birdbath. I can already see a potential problem unless we want all our bird friends to be exterminated.

April 22.   Kitty has fleas! I noticed him constantly scratching and licking an area on his hindquarters. On close examination I saw some black specks. The vet confirmed it was fleas. So I bought some flea powder and vacuumed several times around the area where he sleeps and plays most often. But I know I probably missed some of the pests. We'll probably have to get an exterminator.

April 30.   The fleas finally seem to be gone—and Kitty has stopped scratching. From now on I'll comb her and dust her with flea powder before she comes in after an outing. I don't want to go through this again!

May 14.   Jenny has started trying to train Kitty to sit and heel. She's using an instruction book I picked up at the bookstore. I'm not optimistic. It's slow going, and I'm not really convinced that cats can learn these tricks as well as dogs. At least Jenny seems to be having fun, and she's keeping busy.

May 25. I was wrong! Kitty actually sits many times when Jenny commands him. The use of catnip can work wonders to motivate a cat!

July 6. Kitty got sick yesterday. He had been nibbling on some of our houseplants, and soon afterward he began to throw up. I was afraid that he might be seriously poisoned. We rushed him to the vet, but learned that he's going to be all right. Apparently he swallowed only a small bit of the leaves on the plants.

So what do we do about the plants? We could try to train the cat to stay away from them, but I'm worried that might not work soon enough to protect his health. I guess we'll just have to put the plants outside and hope the cat doesn't eat them when we take him for an outing.

September 20. Kitty went outside without his leash and decided to jump over the fence and go off for an adventure on his own. Jenny cried for a solid hour because she was sure the cat wouldn't return.

He did come back later that afternoon, but there was reason for her to worry. Our peaceable pet had gotten into a fight, probably with one of the stray cats that roams around here. He certainly got the worst of the encounter, with a bloody ear, scratches several places on his body, and wads of hair torn off. We got him to the vet immediately.

September 21.   Fortunately Kitty was up-to-date on all his shots, so we don't have to worry about rabies, feline leukemia, or any of those diseases. But the vet thought that one of the bite marks was deep enough to warrant some antibiotics. So we'll have to give him pills for the next few days to prevent an infection and possible abscess.

September 22.   I decided to give Jenny the task of administering the antibiotic pills. She just turned ten, and she feels she's up to the job. In fact she did really well, probably better than I would have done.

She put Kitty up on a low table, wrapped him loosely in a towel so that he was completely covered except for his head, and began to stroke him carefully. Then she tilted his head up toward the ceiling and pressed gently on the side of each jaw, so that he opened his mouth. When the mouth opened, she popped in a pill and blew on his nose. He immediately swallowed, and the job was done!

CHAPTER TWELVE

IS THERE AN ANIMAL HEAVEN?

IS THERE AN ANIMAL HEAVEN? Nobody knows, of course, but plenty of cat owners *hope* there is because they would like nothing better than to spend an eternity with their pets.

Despite the nine-lives myth, the lifespan of a long-lived cat is about eighteen years. That means that few will outlive their owners, unless the cat was acquired when the human caretaker was quite old. Consequently, at some point you'll have to prepare for the departure of your pet from this earth.

What can you expect during the painful period of separation?

When a Pet Passes Away

The process of confronting the death of a pet is similar to that of confronting the death of any loved one, including a human. The closer you are to your pet, the more your grieving and mourning responses will approximate the death of any family member.

Many death and grief experts have commented on the stages, phases, or "tasks" of mourning. I like to divide the experience into *dying* and *death* because there do seem to be two separate emotional attitudes that characterize the two events: In other words, you tend to go through one set of responses when your pet is terminally ill, and another when he actually dies. Many times the death may occur so quickly, as in a traffic accident, that there is no time to deal with the dying process. Other times, though, the pet becomes seriously ill, and handling the dying experience becomes an important challenge.

In a classic formulation in her book *On Death and Dying,* Dr. Elisabeth Kübler-Ross suggests the following five stages in dealing with dying:

- Denial and isolation. You simply can't believe or accept the fact that the loved one is going to die.
- Anger. You accept the inevitability of death, but you become angry at yourself, God, the pet, or some other target. Also, you may start assigning blame: "So-and-so didn't watch the cat closely enough, and that's why she got outside and was killed by that car."
- Bargaining. You begin to negotiate for the recovery of the pet. For example, you may try to make a "deal" with God: "If you let Tabby live, I'll do thus and so."
- Depression. You realize the bargaining isn't going to work, and now everything seems hopeless. You wonder how you'll ever recover from this loss.

- Acceptance. You finally realize that at some
  point your pet had to die, and you know
  that somehow you'll be able to make it
  through the grief process and get on with
  your life.

Kübler-Ross came up with these stages after observing
the dying of human patients, but the points apply quite
well to pets, such as cats. Similarly, when a cat actually
dies, there are certain responses that can be expected.

Colin Murray Parkes defines four phases of mourning
that occur after the death of a loved human being—the
same occur at the loss of a pet:

- Numbness. In a sense you're emotionally an-
  esthetized for a short time just after the
  death occurs. The full reality of the loss
  hasn't registered yet.
- Yearning. You want desperately for the dead
  cat to return, and you somehow can't accept
  the fact of the death. You also become
  angry.
- Disorganization and despair. You have trouble putting your life in order or functioning
  effectively after the death. There is confusion
  and an inability to perform even ordinary
  daily tasks because of preoccupation with the
  death.
- Rebuilding your life. You finally accept the
  death and begin to reorganize yourself so
  that you can function again.

Dr. J. William Worden, in his respected text *Grief Counseling and Grief Therapy,* describes the response to a death
in terms of "tasks." He believes that this approach helps

the individual and the health practitioner to take practical action to deal with the death process. The four tasks identified by Worden, and my accommodation of them to your pet, include the following:

- Accepting the reality of the loss. You have to go beyond numbness or denial of death and recognize that your cat has indeed left you— for good.
- Experiencing the pain of grief. Too often those who have lost a pet refuse to face their feelings, or they deny the presence of pain.
- Adjusting to an environment without the pet. It can be tough to sit in the same room where your cat once hopped about, rubbed against your legs, or rested in your lap. Your companion is now gone, and you have to get on with your life by finding new activities and attitudes to fill the void, and perhaps eventually adopting a new cat.
- Investing your emotional energy in another relationship.

One of the best ways to get over the loss of any companion is to substitute another satisfying relationship as soon as possible. This principle applies to pets as well as to humans.

Replacing Your Pet

If a romantic relationship or marriage ends, eventually you will rejoin society and find another girlfriend, boyfriend, or spouse. Similarly, if your cat dies, you should consider getting another cat as soon as possible. The responsibility of caring for a new kitten, helping him adjust to your home, and reorganizing your environment to make him comfortable will lessen the grief over your dead pet.

Should you try to acquire a cat as much like your former one as possible? You'll never find another animal who will precisely fill the role of the previous cat. Pets, like humans, are not interchangeable.

In addition, if you obtain a cat that looks similar, you will always be comparing your new cat to the deceased one. The relationship with the new pet will suffer because you'll think, "Kitty didn't behave this way." Or, "Kitty always loved this food—why won't *he* eat it?" Or even, "Why don't you sit in my lap the way Kitty did?" Finally, you may get angry with the new pet because it's not behaving just like the old one.

So I would recommend that you forget about trying to replace your first pet with a kind of replica. Just look for another cat that appeals to you and seems a good fit for your personality and household. It will be helpful if the new one is a completely different breed and bears no physical resemblance to the prior pet. The chances are good that even a cat with a new look and personality will quickly become a part of your life and help you move beyond grief.

What About the Reactions of Other Members of Your Household—Including Other Pets?

Other human members of your household will most likely react to the death of the cat in the same way you do. Their attachment to the pet will determine just how intensely they mourn or grieve.

As for other pets, the responses to the death of a companion pet can be quite varied. If you have two cats who are quite close and get along with each other well, the loss of one can have serious repercussions for the survivor. The remaining cat may become quite depressed and often seem to be looking around for the other animal. He knows his friend is gone, but he can't understand that he won't return.

On the other hand, if the pets were rivals or enemies, the survivor may not care at all that the dead one is gone. In fact his personality may change for the better!

In any case, when you replace the dead pet with another one, the dynamics of pet interactions will change. The presence of the "new cat on the block" will immediately transform the relationships, and most likely any depression on the part of a pet survivor will disappear. However, if you do get a new cat, take the time to properly introduce the animals to one another.

How to Talk to an Owner Whose Cat Has Died

Those who don't have a pet often can't understand how devastated an owner can be when an animal companion dies. For that matter even pet owners who have not experienced a pet death can be insensitive.

It's important *not* to tell the owner-survivor, "Oh, he was just an animal." Or, "You can get another pet." That's somewhat like telling the parent of a child who has passed away, "Oh, he was just a little kid." Or, "You can always have another child."

Remember, in many ways cats *are* people, at least to their owners. They provide companionship, therapy, and many other functions, particularly to those who otherwise live alone.

Many times when I speak with individuals whose pets have died years before, the memory of the pet is still sharp, as though that pet just died yesterday. The grief process may be over in a few weeks, especially if the owner has acted swiftly to replace the animal. But in some cases the mourning may go on in some form for months or even years.

So it's important as you're dealing with a friend who has lost a cat to ascertain how that person feels and what his needs are. Be content to be a good listener, and don't insist on providing a lot of advice. Be sympathetic. If your friend wants advice, mention some of the points I've outlined about the mourning and grieving process. Then let him decide what seems useful and pertinent to his particular situation.

I've had contact with individuals years after their pet has died, and somehow a part of the pain is still there. Many times, they begin to cry. In those moments I listen and learn a great deal about the bond between owner and pet. If this happens to you, ask the grieving owner to tell you funny stories about the pet. Let the owner cry if he feels like it, and a hug or pat on the shoulder always helps. Also, if *your* pet passes away, don't be ashamed to cry and grieve. It's normal to mourn the loss.

When you think about your pet in a sad moment, remember how much richer your life was for having had him as part of your life. Always recall the joy and happiness your cat gave you. When you ponder those experiences, a smile may come onto your face and you'll feel much better.

Is It Ever Appropriate to Help Your Pet Pass On?

The question of euthanasia—the mercy killing of a pet that is terminally ill or in too much agony to live—has always been an issue among pet owners. There are no ironclad rules that can be laid down on the subject. Certainly "putting a pet to sleep" when he is in tremendous pain and there is no hope of recovery is the kind, reasonable thing to do. But there are many other situations that involve more difficult decisions.

For example, suppose you have a pet with a heart condition, which the vet says will eventually lead to disability and death *unless* the problem is treated. But the treatment may involve surgery or a pacemaker, which will be costly and may only prolong the cat's life for a few months. What should you do?

The personal philosophy of the owner, his budget, and various other considerations must come into play in making a decision. So long as you act in a way that is consistent with your moral and ethical values and your financial means, you can rest assured that you've done all that is humanly—or felinely—possible.

CONCLUSION: YES, CATS *DO* HAVE NINE LIVES!

CATS, perhaps more than any other type of pet, really do seem to have extra dimensions to their lives. In fact rather fortuitously I've been able to identify nine of those dimensions. In a sense your cat may be able to enjoy these nine full lives—so long as you, the owner, help him.

LIFE #1: CATS ARE SURVIVORS

The myth of a cat's having nine lives undoubtedly arose in part because cats are unusually adept at getting out of tight, often life-threatening situations. Cats really have fallen four stories or more and then stood up and walked away without a scratch. They have the ability to land on their feet—quite literally—in circumstances that would have resulted in the death of a human or another animal.

Also, they are wily, agile creatures with the instincts of a natural hunter. They are alert to opportunities, as well as to dangers, and their ability to react quickly, such as by climbing out of the reach of enemies on the ground, adds to their survival potential.

In short, cats are survivors—and that accounts for one way that they can last longer than many other creatures.

LIFE #2: CATS ARE NATURAL COMPANIONS

Among some people cats have the reputation for being aloof or unfriendly and not particularly interested in establishing relationships with other animals or people. But cat owners know better. They know cats can be great companions. That's why they are the most popular pet.

Because cats have an uncanny ability to establish deep relationships with humans, they have been able to benefit from the advantages conferred by living with owners and being cared for by them. That means that unlike many less fortunate or undomesticated animals, they haven't had to worry about getting enough food or having a secure home and good medical care. Hence they have gained another "life."

LIFE #3: CATS LOVE EXERCISE

Like humans, cats need regular, vigorous exercise to achieve maximum health and life. Otherwise they become obese, their muscles get flabby, their energy levels decline, and they probably become susceptible to more diseases, including heart disease.

To enhance their cat's ability to achieve those nine lives, owners need to let their cats do what they like to do naturally. They need to be out walking, running, or otherwise developing their aerobic capacity.

LIFE #4: CATS ARE SMART—AND ABLE TO BE EDUCATED

Contrary to many popular notions, cats *can* be trained. They can learn to sit, heel, fetch, and perform other feats. Some of these areas of education can be important for their safety and health. For example, training a cat to heel or come when called can lower the risk that he'll run in front of a passing car when you're outdoors. Teaching him to stay away from poisonous plants has obvious benefits.

So even if your cat seems uninterested at first, don't give up on giving your pet a little "higher education." The results will pay off in big benefits, by creating both a better-behaved cat and also one who is able to protect himself from risky situations.

LIFE #5: CATS THRIVE IN A CLEAN ENVIRONMENT

Owners who pay close attention to their cat's litter box, who provide clean eating dishes, and who help older cats groom and clean themselves when the animals aren't able to do a good job will enhance the health of their pets. Such care will also increase the pet's potential for longevity.

LIFE #6: CATS CAN LIVE LONGER WITH CAREFUL MEDICAL ATTENTION

The possibility of a longer life is *greatly* improved when the owner establishes a solid relationship with a vet and immediately contacts the vet for treatment when the cat is sick or injured.

This interaction with the animal doctor will also lead to proper vaccinations, nutritional guidance, and other preventive measures that will give the cat at least one more "extra life."

LIFE #7: CATS TEND TO LIVE LONGER IN A LOW-RISK ENVIRONMENT

When you thoroughly cat-proof your home—taking such precautions as locking up medicines and chemicals and removing poisonous plants from the home—you'll greatly lower the risk that your pet will be hurt or killed by accident.

Also, appropriate use of cat equipment, such as a leash when the cat is in a potentially dangerous environment outdoors, can keep a cat's life from being cut tragically off.

LIFE #8: CATS CAN ADAPT

As we've seen in the previous pages, with an owner's help a cat can easily learn to travel long distances, move to strange locations, and adjust to changes in the living environment, such as may happen with the arrival of a new baby or pet.

In short, cats are adaptable. This ability to roll with the punches gives them an edge in living a longer and happier life.

LIFE #9: CATS RESPOND TO LOVE

In a sense this ninth "life" has been implied in all the others. The unusually strong cat might live a long time without an owner's love, but *most* cats thrive best on affection and caring attention.

The presence of an obviously compassionate and concerned owner will translate into a more secure, emotionally well-adjusted cat. Also, love tends to drive out fear, stress, and other negative forces that can impair health and shorten life. The cat who is loved is the cat who will live fully and abundantly—and will realize that legendary ability to enjoy nine full lives.

To live with your cat, then, means to live *for* him. It means to care for him, to place his welfare on a high plane, to treat him as a genuine member of the household. He has feelings that must be respected and needs that must be satisfied. Most important of all, he has the capacity to give and receive love, and it's up to you as a kind of surrogate parent to establish the context where that natural human-pet affection can grow and flourish.

APPENDIX

This appendix consists of a couple of practical forms to help you care more effectively for your pet:

I. A weekly log, which will enable the owner to organize the cat's day and keep track of important exercise, dietary, and hygienic information.

I would suggest that you decide in advance on the times you want your cat to do certain things and also on the types and amounts of his food and other items. Then, at the end of the day, indicate the actual way that the tasks or responsibilities were performed.

II. A section for recording medical records, including visits to the vet, vaccinations, illnesses, and reactions to various medications.

III. As I mentioned in Chapter Eleven, I recommend that every owner also buy a daily diary to record events in the cat's life more extensively. You might want to begin the diary with such important information as your cat's pedigree and a description that includes special markings (so that you can describe him accurately if lost) and even a photograph. After that the journal is yours to record any and all memorable events—both highlights and low spots—that both you and your cat encounter.

I. Weekly Cat Log

DAY 1

Sleeping habits:

Time to bed:
Time awake:
Naps:
Comments:

Meals eaten, including times and amounts:

Morning:
Evening:
Other:
Comments (including identification of caretaker who did the feeding):

Litter box habits:

Frequency of urination:
Frequency of bowel movements:

Box cleaned (daily)?
Litter changed (weekly)?
Comments (including caretaker's name):

Exercise:

Type:
Amount:
Comments (including caretaker who accompanied cat):

Cat's appointments:

Other daily events or concerns:

Amusing events:

Experiences with parents, friends, relatives, and children:

Experiences with other animals:

DAY 2

Sleeping habits:

Time to bed:
Time awake:
Naps:
Comments:

Meals eaten, including times and amounts:

Morning:
Evening:
Other:
Comments (including identification of caretaker who did the feeding):

Litter box habits:

Frequency of urination:
Frequency of bowel movements:
Box cleaned (daily)?
Litter changed (weekly)?
Comments (including caretaker's name):

Exercise:

Type:
Amount:
Comments (including caretaker who accompanied cat):

Cat's appointments:

Other daily events or concerns:

Amusing events:
Experiences with parents, friends, relatives, and children:
Experiences with other animals:

D A Y 3

Sleeping habits:

Time to bed:
Time awake:
Naps:
Comments:

Meals eaten, including times and amounts:

Morning:
Evening:
Other:

Comments (including identification of caretaker who did the feeding):

Litter box habits:

Frequency of urination:
Frequency of bowel movements:
Box cleaned (daily)?
Litter changed (weekly)?
Comments (including caretaker's name):

Exercise:

Type:
Amount:
Comments (including caretaker who accompanied cat):

Cat's appointments:

Other daily events or concerns:

Amusing events:
Experiences with parents, friends, relatives, and children:
Experiences with other animals:

DAY 4

Sleeping habits:

Time to bed:
Time awake:
Naps:
Comments:

Meals eaten, including times and amounts:

Morning:
Evening:
Other:
Comments (including identification of caretaker who did the feeding):

Litter box habits:

Frequency of urination:
Frequency of bowel movements:
Box cleaned (daily)?
Litter changed (weekly)?
Comments (including caretaker's name):

Exercise:

Type:
Amount:
Comments (including caretaker who accompanied cat):

Cat's appointments:

Other daily events or concerns:

Amusing events:
Experiences with parents, friends, relatives, and children:
Experiences with other animals:

DAY 5

Sleeping habits:

Time to bed:
Time awake:
Naps:
Comments:

Meals eaten, including times and amounts:

Morning:
Evening:

Other:
Comments (including identification of caretaker who did the feeding):

Litter box habits:

Frequency of urination:
Frequency of bowel movements:
Box cleaned (daily)?
Litter changed (weekly)?
Comments (including caretaker's name):

Exercise:

Type:
Amount:
Comments (including caretaker who accompanied cat):

Cat's appointments:

Other daily events or concerns:

Amusing events:
Experiences with parents, friends, relatives, and children:
Experience with other animals:

DAY 6

Sleeping habits:

Time to bed:
Time awake:
Naps:
Comments:

Meals eaten, including times and amounts:

Morning:
Evening:
Other:
Comments (including identification of caretaker who did the feeding):

Litter box habits:

Frequency of urination:
Frequency of bowel movements:
Box cleaned (daily)?
Litter changed (weekly)?
Comments (including caretaker's name):

Exercise:

Type:
Amount:
Comments (including caretaker who accompanied cat):

Cat's appointments:

Other daily events or concerns:

Amusing events:
Experiences with parents, friends, relatives, and children:
Experiences with other animals:

DAY 7

Sleeping habits:

Time to bed:
Time awake:
Naps:
Comments:

Meals eaten, including times and amounts:

Morning:
Evening:
Other:
Comments (including identification of caretaker who did the feeding):

Litter box habits:

Frequency of urination:
Frequency of bowel movements:
Box cleaned (daily)?
Litter changed (weekly)?
Comments (including caretaker's name):

Exercise:

Type:
Amount:
Comments (including caretaker who accompanied cat):

Cat's appointments:

Other daily events or concerns:

Amusing events:
Experiences with parents, friends, relatives, and children:
Experiences with other animals:

II. Medical Records

Visits to Veterinarian:

Name of doctor(s):
Address(es) of doctor(s):
Dates and reasons for visits:

Types, dates, and symptoms of illnesses:

Medications prescribed:
Side effects or other reactions:

Vaccinations (types, dates):

Epilogue

When a book is over, it is supposed to be over—but this one isn't.

During much of the time that I was writing this book, I did not own a cat. I had decided that cats were not what I needed during this stage of my life and I adore my dog, Scruffette, and that was enough.

. . . then came the day we had to shoot the cover of *Living with Cats*.

Bob Aulicino, the art director at William Morrow, wanted several cats on the cover with me. Great. Several cats (the cats getting along could be a problem), in a strange location, (that could be a bigger problem, especially if marking territory began) and me in the middle (oh, no). What a challenge, and no guarantees that I would come out alive from the photo shoot. Jamie, my producer, came up with the brilliant suggestion of using kittens. They were the most likely to get along with each other. So where do you find several kittens and cats on the same day?

I called the local animal shelters with which I have worked for years with *Living with Animals:* Montgomery, Washington Humane, and Arlington. They all had cats and kittens and were placed on stand-by. In other words, if the cats and kittens from one shelter were adopted, we would go to the other shelter to get them, and so forth.

The day finally arrived. Several kittens lucked out; they had been adopted. The ones that were left were brought to the photo session. We ended up using cats and kittens from all three shelters. The total was nine kittens and four cats over a two-day period. Even though the plan worked, I got clawed, scratched, and bitten throughout the shoot. Each time we brought in another cat, I was clawed again. One of my outfits that had shoulder pads was the only one that my skin survived. There was one scratch on my hand that seemed to become a magnet for all claws, regardless of size or age. By the end of the first day my back, shoulder, hands, wrist, chest, and legs had taken on the appearance of a war zone. But we all had a great time and confirmed what we already knew, that it is difficult to work with several different cats at the same time!

To top all of this off, there was this one particular four-month-old kitten who showed extraordinary talent and personality. He was with us for both days. He was playful, posed for the camera, stayed in my arms, didn't use his claws at all, and was thrilled with the cat toys. He was affectionate to the many humans who were participating in the shoot and seemed to be careful when he played with the younger kittens.

As the day progressed, the photographer started kidding me about adopting this cat by saying things like, "What if William Morrow chooses this cat for the book cover, and the cat is dead because you didn't adopt it?" And, "Gale, you need this cat. Scruff needs this cat. Your house and life need this cat!" In my hard-hearted, I'm-not-about-to-be-swayed fashion and having worked with animals for nine years, I simply said, "I don't want a cat. You adopt it."

At the end of the first day we took the cat back to the Arlington shelter. As we drove, the photographer kept up the pressure, laughing all the while.

We got to the shelter and took the kitten out of the carrying case. I found myself holding the kitten one more time. Then suddenly I found myself filling out adoption papers, promising to have this kitten neutered when he was old enough, saying, "Yes, I understand how difficult cats can be at first. Yes, if I don't want her I will return her, whoops, him, back to the shelter where I adopted him."

I looked into the eyes of this kitten and said, "So what is so special about you? Why am I adopting you? You have six toes, white paws, and pretty standard coloring. You even have a little white stripe on the tip of your nose!" The shelter director, whom I have known for years, strongly suggested that I take a twenty-four-hour cooling-off period. People who work in shelters are great. They absolutely do not want anyone adopting animals who doesn't want an animal or who will ignore it.

I left the shelter and found myself driving to a pet store to purchase litter, a litter box, and cat food and trying to think of a name. Though I was complaining out loud the whole time, I was inwardly solidifying my adoption of this wonderful kitten. Now the new cat owner in me kicked in. I took the kitten without a name into the pet store in his carrier. At the cat food section I took the kitten out of the carrier and let him choose which food he wanted. Sure enough, the kitten put both paws on one particular bag of cat food and ignored the rest. (Am I becoming weird or what?)

Then it was on to the litter boxes. I placed him in one—

it was too small, even for this kitten. I placed him in the next box, which seemed huge, and it was just right. Then it was on to the collars, leashes, and ID tags. (Yes, I will teach this cat to take walks.) I got her, I mean him, a red collar and gold walking leash.

Now for a name. This was a challenge. I couldn't name it Catette because it is a boy. I was going nuts—Fred, Stop, Cat, Yield, Hey You, Probe, King Henry—brother. Nothing fit. Then suddenly it came, near the end of the second shoot day: Curmudgeon, after my editor Andy Dutter; Cattywhompus, after Tom the photographer, Nemec, after me. I call him Crudge. I know.

I promised myself I would not adopt a cat, yet my own book worked on me. Talk about full circle.

Crudge is already recognizing his name. He is coming to me when I call him, doesn't use his claws, and is ever so gentle. I'm sure *sit, stay, fetch,* and *catch* will be in his vocabulary soon. We are already exercising together.

Scruffette and Crudge are getting along better by the minute. This morning I woke up with Crudge at my head and Scruff at my feet. I can't believe this. I have a cat with six toes, a terrific personality, and a catchy name. Crudge, Scruffette, and I are all adjusting to feeding schedules, attention, time, and discipline. I'm learning something new about myself—I have patience!

By the way, Crudge did make the cover and is the cat that appears to be jumping off my left foot!

BIBLIOGRAPHY

Angel, Jeremy. *Cats' Kingdom*. London: Souvenir Press Limited, 1988.

Baker, Stephen. *How to Live with a Neurotic Cat*. New York: Warner Communications Company, 1985.

Bell, Charles. *First Aid and Health Care for Cats*. New York: Berkley Books, 1991.

Berwick, Ray. *Training Your Cat*. Tucson, Ariz. HP Books, 1986.

Burkholder, Craton. *Emergency Care for Cats and Dogs: First Aid for Your Pet*. New York: Michael Kesend Publishing, Ltd., 1987.

Eckstein, Warren and Fay. *How to Get Your Cat to Do What You Want*. New York: Villard Books, Random House, Inc., 1990.

Fox, Michael W. *The New Animal Doctor's Answer Book*. New York: Newmarket Press, 1984.

————. *Supercat: Raising the Perfect Feline Companion*. New

York: Howell Book House, Macmillan Publishing Company, 1990.

———. *Understanding Your Cat*. New York: Bantam, 1977.

———., and Gates, Wende Devlin. *What Is Your Cat Saying?* Toronto: General Publishing Co., 1982.

Freese, Arthur. *Living Through Grief and Growing with It*. New York: Barnes & Noble Books, Harper & Row, 1977.

Harper's Illustrated Handbook of Cats. New York, Harper & Row, 1985.

Holland, Barbara. *Secrets of the Cat: Its Lore, Legend, and Lives*. New York: Ballantine Books, 1989.

Kay, William J. *The Complete Book of Cat Health*. New York: Macmillan Publishing Company, 1985.

Kübler-Ross, Elisabeth. *On Death and Dying*. New York: Macmillan Publishing Company, 1969.

McCormick, Malachi. *Cat Tales*. New York: Clarkson N. Potter, 1989.

Siegal, Mordecai, ed. *The Cornell Book of Cats: A Comprehensive Medical Reference for Every Cat and Kitten*. New York: Villard Books, Random House, Inc., 1989.

Worden, J. William. *Grief Counseling and Grief Therapy: A Handbook for the Mental Health Practitioner*. New York, Springer Publishing Company, 1982.

Worden, J. William, and Proctor, William. *PDA—Personal Death Awareness*. Englewood Cliffs, N.J.: Prentice-Hall, 1976.

INDEX

PRAISE *for*

THE TRUMPET LESSON

"An adventure of the heart set in the heart of Mexico: Guanajuato, the historic city of music and books, Diego Rivera's childhood home, and rocket blasts into dazzling blue skies, a place where an avocado might hit you on the head or a papaya squish underfoot! Romain knows the secrets and wonders of this UNESCO World Heritage site, and she tells the story of Callie Quinn with aplomb."

—C.M. MAYO, author of *The Last Prince of the Mexican Empire*

"Romain spins a tale of flight from truth-telling—truth-telling to others, truth-telling to one's own heart—and of the harm this can do. Finely crafted, sensitively written, it is a story that will generate self-reflection."

—THOMAS M. ROBINSON, DLitt, DSLitt, Professor Emeritus of Philosophy and Classics, University of Toronto, and author of *Plato's Psychology*

"In this remarkable first novel, you will find yourself looking into your own secrets, lies, and losses as you journey with Callie, both internally and in the streets of Guanajuato, Mexico. Trust, honesty, family, loyalty, shame, and the power of music and love are sensitively explored in *The Trumpet Lesson* with elegant writing and deep empathy for the unusual cast of characters."

—JUDITH JENYA, JD, MSW, founding director of Global Children's Organization and former adoption attorney

"With humor and exquisite tenderness, Dianne Romain vibrantly depicts the city of Guanajuato, the complexity of the human heart, and the struggle to forge true home and family. *The Trumpet Lesson* is really a lesson in loving and being loved. Prepare to be charmed."

—STEPH KILEN, freelance writer and adjunct lecturer,
Carroll University

"As an adoptive mother I know the joy, profound loss, and gratitude that connects adoptive and birth families—a complexity of relationship honestly explored in *The Trumpet Lesson*."

—SARAH LOVETT, author of the Dr. Sylvia Strange series

"*The Trumpet Lesson* follows midwesterner Callie Quinn as she seeks to 'find her inner trumpeter' while living in Guanajuato, Mexico. While struggling to learn a new instrument, Callie also ponders whether she should tell the world—or at least her closest friends—about secrets from her past. Guanajuato itself is also a star of the book, with its narrow and twisty *callejón* walkways, sparkling plazas, and the allure of its local mummies. Romain has written a thoroughly engrossing novel about family, friendships, music, and personal growth. A fantastic read!"

—TIM HEDLUND, banjo player and designer

"A beautiful story of a woman adapting to a foreign land, *The Trumpet Lesson* breathes with the authentic atmosphere of Guanajuato, colorful characters, how a trumpet lesson feels, musical lives, and plenty of philosophy. Bravo!"

—JOHN URNESS, soloist and principal trumpet of the State of
Mexico Symphony Orchestra